GenX and God

A GenX Perspective

GenX and God

A GenX Perspective

KRISTOFFER COX

TEKNA BOOKS
Chanhassen, Minnesota

GENX AND GOD
A GenX Perspective

Publisher's Cataloging-in-Publication
(Provided by Quality Books, Inc.)

Cox, Kristoffer, 1968-
  GenX and God : a GenX perspective / Kristoffer Cox. —
1st ed.
    p. cm.
  Includes bibliographical references and index.
  Preassigned LCCN: 98-90387
  ISBN: 0-9664413-0-3

  1. Generation X—Religious life. 2. Jesus Christ—Significance.
  3. Intergenerational relations. I. Title.
  II. Title: Generation X and God III. Title: GenX and God

BV4529.2.C69 1998   243
                                     QBI98-786

04 03 02 01 00 99 98   8 7 6 5 4 3 2 1

Published by Tekna Books:
http://www.teknabooks.com

Printed in the USA by Morris Publishing
3212 East Highway 30, Kearney, NE 68847
1-800-650-7888

To Rebecca — You are truly a gift from God.

Contents

Foreword

I am honored and excited to write the foreword for this book. I am also a little surprised, because in our society, it is becoming increasingly unusual for aging Boomers like myself to engage in serious dialogue and reflection with members of Kris Cox's generation. Fortunately, Kris has provided a timely invitation and a provocative platform for members of all generations to examine or re-examine their relationship with God and with each other.

Through reading this book, I increased my understanding of the diverse and often misunderstood Generation X. In his opening chapters, Kris lays out in simple and direct language (a refreshing characteristic of today's GenX writers) the realities of his generation. In the process, he presents his generation's overall attitude and approach to life. It's hard to find fault with his views. Many people in Kris' generation formed their basic value system in the aftermath of Watergate, the Iranian hostage situation, hyper-inflation and the Reagan presidency. And today, many of these same Xers feel unnoticed, undervalued, and under pressure to clean up the mess that their well meaning parents and other elders are leaving behind as their legacy. This has led Xers to search for relevant answers to the question, "What's the point?" For too long, we've avoided looking in the mirror of GenX for fear of what we might see. In this book, Kris has cleaned the mirror for us. It's time we take a look.

But even more importantly, Kris provides a ground-breaking, Christ-centered theology for his generation. In his understandable and relevant presentation, he invites his own generation to focus on God's spectacular gifts of love, faith, and grace, and what they mean in our lives. Kris believes, as do I, that his generation has the unique opportunity to become leaders in rejecting the materialistic focus of our current society, replacing it with a much richer and more spiritually rewarding God-centered focus. He hits this home at the end of each chapter with wonderful "Reflection Sections" where readers can incorporate this revolutionary spiritual focus into their everyday lives.

While speaking directly to GenX's spiritual and material concerns, this book also spans generational chasms and thrusts us in the hopeful direction of intergenerational reconciliation. Kris is reflecting theologically on what many of us in the Intentional Intergenerational Ministry movement are feeling— that our world and many of our lives are terribly out of balance. During the 1992 elections, the slogan was "It's the economy stupid!" Kris is telling us "It's God!!"

To get ourselves back into balance we need to listen. We need to open-up ourselves and yield control to God. We can't possibly do this while we are in bondage to the projects of this world. We desperately need God's freeing message. May all generations be entrusted to carry it to the world in unity! What a wonderful challenge!

- *Dr. James Gambone*

Dr. James Gambone currently coordinates the Intentional Intergenerational Ministry Project sponsored by Lutheran Brotherhood (see their website at www.intgenmin.com). During the six years prior to the publication of this book, he has conducted approximately 50 intergenerational dialogues across the United States in churches, community settings and corporations. These dialogues challenge five generations to respectfully listen to each other on important issues and then to develop concrete recommendations for action that are mutually acceptable.

Acknowledgments

This section cannot possibly be long enough! Thank you to everyone who helped in this "project." Especially...

My Creator—for lovingly and mercifully looking beyond my iniquities. My wife Rebecca—my encourager and theological partner in this writing. Thanksgiving! Lutheran Church—for planting seeds in me and for watering and nurturing what grew. Dr. James Gambone and the people of the Intentional Intergenerational Ministry movement—for opening my eyes to the importance of intergenerational reconciliation. My colleagues and friends who were superb editors and sounding boards: Jason Beckman, Chris Cranbrook, Scott Gilsrud, Lee Hallstrom, Claudia and Steve Jordan, Lisa and Tony Kim, Brian Mundt, Roy Noel, Vance Rains, and Michael Sanford. My Godly teachers and seminary professors—most directly influencing this writing were Gerhard Forde, Ernie Gulner, Roland Martinson, Michael Rogness, and Mark Throntveit.

Introduction

I fall into the class of people affectionately (or not) labeled *Generation X*. We *Xers* are the roughly 46 million people born between 1965 and 1985 (largely the children of the Baby Boomers, and not to be confused with the generation following us – the Millennials).[1] But really, the basis of this classification is more an attitude than a birth year. Most people who are older than us can't seem to peg our attitude. That's why they've given us a meaningless title like *X*. This book is written for anyone who might have this elusive "GenX" attitude. I explore this attitude a little more in the first chapter, but it usually includes healthy measures of realism, pessimism, and pain, and is sometimes paradoxically mixed with a measure of hope. This attitude in life stems largely from two circumstances: (1) many of us were not given much hope by our surrounding world during our formative years, and (2) we face a tenuous future. Certainly, most people, regardless of their generation, can relate to these challenges in some way.

My purpose in writing this book is to present to you something that has become very valuable to me, simply because I believe you too might find it to be valuable. As the title of this book hints, this "something" is the living God, who loves us, is very much concerned for us, and is actively involved in our world. Questions about our creation and existence have regained relevance for people today, as our increased knowledge about the cosmos has significantly heightened our awareness of how little we really do know. In other words, our investigation of the universe has largely led us to the infinite. As an Xer, I have spent a lot of time contemplating the universe, the existence of God, what or who that God is, et cetera. Although I write from a Christian perspective, I realize that we might be from different religious traditions and that our understandings of God probably differ. I sincerely hope I have respected any differences in this book, and I hope that regardless of your vantage point, you will find value in what lies in the pages ahead.

Because of the scope and intended perspective of this book, my approach bears a number of presuppositions regarding Christianity as truth. Undoubtedly some readers will develop questions about the reasonableness of Christianity over and against the truth claims of other worldviews. Although I certainly find Christianity to be reasonable, my purpose is not to offer any amount of apologetic "proofs" for the reasonableness of Christianity. This more logical approach is helpful for some but not for others. Regardless, it is well beyond the scope of this book. Those who are interested in further reading in this area should refer to the appendix for a suggested reading list.

The three areas I discuss in this book are: (1) our reality as we typically experience it, (2) the reality of God, and (3) the reality of living life in our world. Each chapter ends with a number of questions for reflection. Readers who spend time with these questions find them to be very helpful—largely because the questions help contextualize the chapters' main points to the unique experiences of each reader. Please consider this fact before skipping them.

Peace be with you!

Part 1

Our Reality

What's the Point?

Nuclear man is the man who realizes that his creative powers hold the potential for self-destruction. He sees such an abundance of material commodities around him that scarcity no longer motivates his life, but at the same time he is groping for a direction and asking for meaning and purpose.[1]

—Henri Nouwen (1932-1996)

We are collectively known as *Generation X*. As individuals we are very diverse, so it is risky to generalize about us. Yet, in the midst of our diversity, we do seem to have a collective attitude toward life. As a generation, it is probably our attitude that defines us best. What is this attitude, and from where did it come? How have our perceptions of the world around us and of our future impacted our attitude and influenced our direction? Recognizing the risks of generalizing, let's take a look at our perceptions. Let's explore the formation of our generation's attitude and approach to life.

While preparing to write this book, I was reading an article about our generation and a strange thing happened. The author of the article, also an Xer, quoted a line from an R.E.M. song that says, "It's the end of the world as we know it (and I feel fine)." This quote in itself is not so odd. After all, it is a song from our era. But what was strange was that as I read this line, I had my headphones on and was listening to that very song! Why is it that this "coincidence" happened? People of every generation share with their peers music common to their generation's unique history. It only makes sense that, as Xers, we too share common music, as we also share a number of common experiences and attitudes. This song by R.E.M. is popular with our generation largely because it somehow reflects some of what we have in common.

All generations have their unique quirks to which people from other generations can't fully relate. But it seems that others have great difficulty identifying with us specifically. We seem to successfully escape the attempts of others to label our generation. Society confirms this by failing to give us any meaningful, positive label. Instead, we are given the generic, multipurpose symbol, *X*. Another label that we are sometimes given is *Baby Busters*. This is an obvious play on the title held by most of our parents who are *Baby Boomers*. But *Buster* is as elusive as *X*. If anything, it sounds like a broken version of *Boomer* and has negative connotations.[2] We are also less-than-affectionately called *Slackers*. This refers to our alleged lack of motivation toward being productive in society. Are we accurately represented by these and other negative terms? I think not! Such labels certainly demonstrate the difficulty others have in understanding us.

Much of this stereotyping was, and still is, market driven. Using a "divide and conquer" methodology, marketers drew somewhat arbitrary lines around us in order to have a defined target at which they could shoot their products in order to make money. The generational divisions resulted in what we now know as GenX. Certainly, we are not the only generation to be raped by the greed of others. But sadly, not having any better ideas, society has fallen right in line with the established paradigm. Because the market-driven approach offers a sense of control, the government, the church, interest groups, and many other institutions have adopted this approach toward us. This fosters intergenerational tension and division, which then raises our anxiety level as we stand before an obstacle-filled future requiring incredible intergenerational cooperation.

What is it that makes us so difficult to peg? Why do our elders continue to treat us as if we're a separate target market at odds with their future rather than of a part of their future? Largely, those older than us can't peg us because they've only recently noticed us. Until now, our elders were quite busy making their marks in the world. Their carefree pursuit of various social freedoms in the 1960's followed by their unforgiving pursuit of the American Dream left us, Generation X, in their dust.

Many of their various quests for "success" have exhausted resources that we will need for our own self-care as well as to care for them as they age. We are the first generation expected to have a lower standard of living than our parents. We have been handed a multi-trillion dollar national debt. Our Social Security and Medicaid systems are financially upside-down. In 1935, there were forty workers for every retiree. By the early 1990's, this number had dropped to 3.4, and it continues to drop today.[3] We face countless environmental instabilities. And these are only a few of the many anxiety-causing concerns of our future.

Moreover, as long as Boomers maintain the societal control that they so covet, Xers will only be allowed to operate within Boomer-prescribed guidelines. For example, the Boomer controlled music industry is why our generation had to find "alternative" ways to produce and market our own music.[4] I ran into similar barriers when trying to get this book published in a Boomer controlled publishing industry. Our nation's decision-making system is no different. Where is our voice and the voice of future generations in politics? Because of their numbers, our elders control political power. Should we then be surprised that legislation often favors interests of the elderly while children under eighteen (who don't vote) are the group with the highest proportion now in poverty? For example, the elderly, who no longer have young children, systematically vote-down educational levies.[5] All of this speaks to the very wide intergenerational chasms in our society.

We have inherited the responsibility to deal with a very challenging future. Yet, we are not empowered with the authority to roll-up our sleeves and meet the challenge. Theologian Jurgen Moltmann addresses this phenomenon,

> Every society has a social contract which it has worked out for itself. But there is a contract between the generations too, and this has not been worked out. Because children are the weakest members, and because coming generations have no say in today's decisions, the costs of present profits are shuffled off on to them.[6]

Now, our parents are aging and are anxious about their future. They realize that they must soon rely on the generation in which they did not personally invest—their own Frankenstein creation—to support them in their old age, and they are scared.

In many respects, the fear of our parents is justified. Especially since in addition to the lack of social investment, the lack of personal investment in our generation is also bearing fruit. We naturally question the authority and guidance of our elders and of society in general, which in our past have born little but false promises. The ideal images such as *Mr. Rogers*, *Leave it to Beaver*, and *The Brady Bunch*, from which we took many of our social clues as young children, were nothing but electronic pacifiers—a far cry from the reality many of us eventually experienced. While our parents were busy climbing

22

corporate ladders or building their own ladders, many of us were in day care and in latchkey programs. Likewise, many of us fended for ourselves in empty homes after school and were sent to summer camps to keep us out from underfoot.[7] Sensitive to the low priority our parents gave us as children, we can see right through their quests for material and professional status, which they claimed were pursued "for our benefit."

Too often, many families dissolved. Close to 50 percent of Xers are from broken or remarried families.[8] Because most marriage vows say something like "until death do us part" rather than "until one or both of us get sick of each other," we can safely assume that many such family situations do not represent desired or optimal outcomes. If our individual families were lucky enough to remain intact, we rarely spent time together. Our most basic relational unit, the family, became expendable. These and similar facets of our upbringings undoubtedly cause us great amounts of pain. Even if some of us were fortunate enough to grow up in nurturing environments, many of our peers were not. Empathizing with their pain, we all share many of the same insights and resulting approaches to life. Our early disillusionment with the false promises of our elders' value systems has left us with apathetic, skeptical, and even revolutionary world-views.

Our resulting views have both positive and negative implications. Positively, they are a defensive reaction against the lack of attention and false promises we have endured. One benefit of being home alone as youth is that we value relationships. We long for real, meaningful relationships, and we are skeptical of people who prefer to remain superficial. False promises have caused us to confront life's institutions, including things such as government, religion, marriage, and even our world's truth-claims, with caution. This caution is quite natural. For example, early in life, the pain we felt when we first burned ourselves on a stove or a cup of hot liquid made its mark. We quickly learned to approach potentially hot objects with a healthy measure of skepticism! This is good! In some ways, we've been burned, and a measure of skepticism is in order.

Another positive implication is that the lack of trust and responsibility given to us has pushed us to a MacGyver-like level of resourcefulness. The spirit of independence and ingenuity permeates our generation on multiple levels,[9] and this spirit is increasing everyday. Our survival instinct is a huge asset for us in the face of the many challenges we will face in the coming years.

However, the false promises and shattered families in our past also work against us, causing us to be "gun-shy." Life not turning out as was advertised has taken its toll, and effects have rippled throughout our generation. One example of this is that children of divorced parents often have difficulty committing to serious relationships, and finally to marriage. The average age for marriage has increased with our generation.[10] It's good that we have the insight to approach relationships and marriage seriously, but I know a number of people who, because of past events in their families, definitely avoid commitment. Being single is certainly respectable, and for many it is ideal. Yet, the experiences that cause Xers to be gun-shy predispose many of us to a life without marriage, and we are unfortunately missing at least the option to enjoy the many riches that can only be found in the actual marriage covenant. Such effects of life not resulting as advertised are widespread, and our relationships are not the only areas that suffer. Our cautious attitudes also impact other commitment areas such as our potential professions and approaches to religion.

While we may sometimes be gun-shy, we often find ourselves in an almost revolutionary mindset. There is an imbalance of power in our society. This imbalance stems from our elders' failure to release to us the authority we need to attack our generation's and society's challenges in a balanced way. But we cannot solely blame our parents for the resulting intergenerational tensions. The standoff is fueled by both sides. For example, one Xer wrote the following two statements:

> The problem Boomers have with the generation that came right after them is what anyone would have upon suddenly noticing that their shadow was talking back to them.[11]

> The attitude that typifies our generation is resistance to, independence from, and a rejection of Boomer cultural "values." Our generation is the one that will utter the truths that Boomers don't want to hear....You don't have to be a black nationalist rap group (or even a fan of one) to see why "Fight the Power" is a reasonable anthem for Generation X. And you don't have to apologize for joining the revolution.[12]

Yes, both sides are fueling the fire. In the years ahead, it might just be that class warfare will be redefined as the young against the old, rather than the poor against the rich.[13]

Where does all this leave us? One scholar labeled us a "clinically depressed generation." Others have called us pessimistic, apathetic, untrusting, and cynical.[14] Almost all labels given to us are not positive. Maybe these labels are true to some degree, and maybe not. The question that we naturally ask is, "So what?" We're not very fond of such labels. Everybody from every generation has events in their past that form them positively and negatively. True, we weren't born into the same *Leave it to Beaver* societal ideals into which many of our parents were born. But, in many ways, the disillusionments and painful events of our unique upbringings as Xers give us much deeper and more realistic insights into life than they ever had! Our standard of living may not reach that of our parents, but does that mean our quality of life must also be lower? While we are a generation subject to many tensions, we are not without hope! All prejudgments and labels aside, we are who we are, and that's where we need to start. But where are we going? Because we live in a rapidly changing era and have many pressures on us from different directions, many of which we inherited (often resulting from our elders' lack of strategic vision), answering these questions is not a simple task.[15]

In the remainder of this book, we will explore our vision and direction as Xers using the question, "What's the point of life?" as our underlying motivator. This question is appropriate for our generation. Our future seems to hang in the balance. We seem to be cut loose from our moorings. In many ways, our direction is blurred. But because we have been set adrift in an age when information flows like never before, we have the advantage of a more objective (although sometimes overwhelming) view of our situations and options in life than previous generations ever had. This allows us, in fact forces us, to rethink some of what were previously held by others as basic presuppositions to life. Big issues such as our purpose in life and the relevance of God surface. We certainly hope for more out of life than simply birth, survival, and eventually death. But having been tossed around in its wake, we do not identify with society's obsession to pursue "success" for its own sake. If this is not our direction, then what is?

Intergenerational tensions like those I have described in my admittedly stereotypical and sometimes harsh language exist in all generations in different forms or degrees. My intention in this chapter was not to demonize our parents or engage in "Boomer-Bashing," but to describe in the best way possible how our intergenerational tensions along with our uncertain future have formed our generation's attitude and approach to life. I also realize that GenX is diverse in thought and that I can't possibly represent the sentiments of all Xers. My hope is that, in this chapter, I adequately presented the tensions surrounding and challenging our generation as a whole.

Let's now press forward and engage our situation in more depth. We know we have been seriously impacted by intergenerational tensions and by our apparently dark future. How have these factors affected our direction? Who are we now, and where are we going? *What's the point?*

Reflections

List some experiences and attitudes you feel are common to your generation.

Looking back, what aspects of your relationships or other situations in life have been... Frustrating? Fulfilling? Painful? Comforting?

How might have intergenerational barriers or tensions affected your life?

What in your future is overwhelming or stressful?

What in your future is exciting or promising?

Where do you find any hope in life?

Chapter Two

Projects

> You have succeeded in making your earthly life so rich and
> varied, that you no longer stand in need of an eternity. Having
> made a universe for yourselves, you are above the need of
> thinking of the universe that made you.[1]
> — *Friedrich Schleiermacher (1768-1834)*

Brian

   Some of Brian's earliest memories are of his
desire to be a pilot. In fact, the first sentence out of his
mouth was, "There it goes!" as he watched an airplane
takeoff at an airport. From the time he was little, Brian
knew that if he could just become a professional pilot, he
would be happy. People in his life affirmed this as a
noble goal, so he set his life in motion toward becoming
a pilot. When Brian was in junior high, he built and flew
radio controlled airplanes. On his sixteenth birthday, he
got a job bagging groceries to pay for flying lessons.
One year later, he earned his private pilot's license.
   Brian went through Air Force ROTC in college,

and majored in a technical degree (although he preferred non-technical stuff) because it would give him an edge when applying for Air Force pilot training. He spent a lot of his time and hard-earned money accumulating special aerobatic flying time. Upon graduating from college, Brian was accepted into the Air Force's elite fighter pilot training school. He had achieved his dream! Just a few months after starting pilot training, though, he found the whole experience to be extremely anti-climactic. His entire life's investment had brought little or no fulfillment. This revelation was a complete shock to him, and it turned his world upside-down. He knew that life in a demanding career for which he was apathetic would be a painful endurance test. So, he eliminated himself from his coveted flying career and cross-trained to another. Brian found that new career to be no more fulfilling, so as soon as he was able, he went back to school to get a different degree.

Why is it that we are preoccupied with finding meaning or happiness in life? Some of us have looked for the "right" career to bring fulfillment. Others look for contentment in financial independence. Some search for happiness in recreation, convinced of the truth of the bumper sticker, "The one who dies with the most toys wins." Whether it's a career, spirituality, contribution to society, recreation, a classic Harley Davidson, or a collection of sticks with peculiar twists, our chase for fulfillment is on!

This search for fulfillment is a universal human occurrence. Why? The most obvious reason is that we are unfulfilled. Otherwise, why would we seek fulfillment? Another way to understand our search is that in reality, it's a diversion from our natural state of unhappiness. This may sound rather depressing, but let's consider it. Question: Why do we go out with friends? Answer: Because we enjoy their company. Question: Why go to movie theaters? Answer: To be entertained. Question: Why do we have hobbies? Answer: To have fun. This list could go on for ever! If we must intentionally do things to have fun or to seek fulfillment, what does this say about our regular condition? Blaise Pascal, the father of the computer and initial designer of Paris' Metro, answers this question with brilliant simplicity; "If our condition were truly happy we should not need to divert ourselves from thinking about it."[2] Pascal's insight from the early 1600s tells us that our need for diversion is not unique to our time! A lack of fulfillment or unhappiness with our lives in this world is a basic aspect of life.

If our need for diversion is real, then our life is really just one big "project," or a combination of projects, for the purpose of living in denial of some undesirable condition. What exactly is this condition? Pulitzer Prize-winning author Ernest Becker proposes that our project is to flee or seek diversion from ourselves. In the interest of self-preservation, we deny the terror of our finite humanity. He says:

> The fear of death must be present behind all our normal functioning, in order for the organism to be armed toward self-preservation. But the fear of death cannot be present constantly in one's mental functioning, else the organism could not function.[3]

We are a strange creation that has a god-like consciousness hopelessly attached to an animal's body. In rather crude terms, each of us is a "god who shits."[4] We are aware of our own splendid uniqueness in that we stick out of nature with a towering majesty, and yet we go back a few feet into the ground in order to blindly and dumbly rot and disappear forever.[5] The prospect of this creaturely death is terrifying! Our projects in life are either to provide the basic necessities in life so that we do not die, or if we are not at immediate risk of dying, they serve to keep ourselves distracted from pondering our inevitable end as food for worms.[6] In either case, it's our finite creatureness that motivates us. In the latter case, it's our creatureness that we prefer to deny!

Today, we may even safely say that many older and physically safer death-*denying* projects are increasingly being replaced with extreme, death-*defying* projects[7] — the ultimate form of denial! Projects of defiance are more frequent than ever. They began ages ago with death-defying events such as gladiator and bull fighting. Although they still intrigue us, our current level of immersion in the extreme has caused such events to lose some of their sensational attraction. In my relatively young memory (I was born in 1968), the list of public extremists begins with Evil Knevil and continues until today when extreme activities are no longer exceptional spectacles, but commonplace. Because defying death is now marketed as a part of everyday life for all to enjoy, we have become numbed. It seems that we must find ways to pump even more adrenaline into our system to keep the buzz going! In our generation, the defiance of death is championed. Trademarks like "No Fear" run rampant. Amusement parks without death-defying rides flop. Soft drink and other advertising campaigns advocate living life on the edge. Bungee jumping, rock-climbing, and sky-boarding are "in." Some media resources are solely dedicated to coverage of "extreme" sports. Even if we don't personally participate in these death-defying projects, we are intrigued watching others do so — living our extreme life vicariously.

Why have we shifted our focus from denial to defiance? My suggestion is that this shift is a symptom of our shifting worldview. As I stated in the previous chapter, Generation X has been handed an obstacle-filled future which hints at instability and challenges our hope. For many, consciously or not, hopefulness relates to life and hopelessness points to death (a quick survey of some of the reasons behind anxiety, depression, and suicide supports this). Rather than rolling over and accepting our apparently hopeless situations and futures, we rebel against them and challenge them. Extreme times seem to call for extreme actions, and what better way to challenge death than to do battle with it and be victorious? Thus, we have our increasing preoccupation with death-defying extreme projects.

Our anti-death projects today certainly get our blood flowing, but projects don't always require an overdose of adrenaline to meet their objective. Let's now look further at how we relate to the less flashy, but no less potent, projects of our parents' generation. In the first chapter, I mentioned that we Xers have effectively rejected our parents' death-denying projects (largely careerism and pursuit of the American Dream). This does not mean that we will refuse to have productive careers if the opportunity to do so presents itself. But it does mean that we recognize some of the pitfalls of letting careers drive, and possibly wreck, our lives. Our astute realization leaves us in a precarious position. We recognize the shortcomings of the projects society has recommended to us and are left to face our creatureness with no ready-made death denying projects to pursue. We certainly try to stir up the waters with our own, more extreme projects, but the bottom line is that mainlining adrenaline can't sustain us forever. The high will eventually wear off and we will crash. Even in waters we have stirred-up with our extreme games, we ultimately find that we are still drifting aimlessly (although our heart may be pounding a little faster) in the reality of our hopeless condition as inevitable food for worms. We cannot seem to find the means to sail out of our situation and on to better things.

We typically react to this dilemma in one of two ways. One way is to dabble in different areas, searching for a worthwhile project and hoping to find more solid ground or a higher meaning somewhere. Such projects might include a course of education, a certain career, a worthy cause, concern for our future, a devotion to religion, or even rebellion against those we feel are oppressing us. In the meantime, we scrape for meaning in relationships and in enjoying life as it unfolds. A second reaction is to throw up our arms in futility, and to simply become apathetic about the meaning of life. Here, unlike the first reaction, we seem to have abandoned our search for an ideal project. We simply enter survival mode, resigning ourselves to finding meaning in our daily lives as we experience them, and having as much fun as possible along the way. In reality, finding meaning through this second type of reaction (we might call it an "anti-project project") then becomes our project.

This result is ironic. Even if we reject society's typical projects, we are not left projectless. Instead, our project becomes either our search for an alternative project, or our treatment of our current situation as our project. This closes the circle around us and society. Our projects may be different from those of our parents and from people of other generations, but we still have them. We are imprisoned by our own attempts, whether half-hearted or sincere, to avoid the trappings into which others, including our parents, have fallen. This realization is frustrating! In spite of our most well intentioned skepticism and defensive measures, we remain trapped.

We have seen that the apparently hopeless reality of our creatureness drives us toward various projects. However, these reality-denying projects simply encircle the same reality from which we are attempting to flee, cutting off all escape routes. What, then, are we to do? Once we realize we're trapped, we feel that we can only do one thing—free ourselves. In order to

34

escape this circle, we eventually seek to somehow transport ourselves outside the circle's boundaries. Our inclination is to look for a new reality — one that is free from the trappings and futilities of our projects. In other words, we realize that we're stuck on a boat with an uncomfortable reality. So, as we are drifting, we naturally look for other boats with different systems of reality to pass us by. We hope that one will pass close enough for us to jump on board.

Reflections

Name some areas where you have searched for meaning or happiness in life.

List some ways in which "the extreme" is promoted in society today.

Why do you think people enjoy activities like "bungee jumping"?

What "projects" do you currently have that give you enjoyment or help fill your day?

Why might people seek to break free from their own "circle" (pages 34-35) of projects?

Think about how the saying "The grass is always greener on the other side of the fence" might relate to our searches for other realities.

Chapter Three

Transcendence

The sole cause of man's unhappiness is that he does not know how to stay quietly in his room. What people want is not the easy peaceful life that allows us to think of our unhappy condition. That is why we prefer the hunt to the capture. That is why we choose some attractive object to entice us in ardent pursuit.[1]

— Blaise Pascal (1623-1662)

Alexis

Alexis has dated a number of different men, but she has not really connected with any of them. The dating scene is definitely getting old. She thinks she might like a serious relationship, but she just hasn't met the right man yet. Three years ago, she had finally found her dream job in the environmental impact division of a large manufacturing corporation. She believes in the cause of her work, but now she's beginning to find the work itself to be pretty dry. Alexis is beginning to think that there must be more to life, so she just enrolled in a community education class titled, "Learn to Unlock Your Inner Spirituality."

37

To use an analogy from the previous chapter, Alexis realizes that she's stuck on a boat. She knows that she's drifting—bound within a circle of projects. Some projects she has intentionally pursued and others exist just due to the nature of life, but none allow her the diversion she would like. Her hope is that she might sight another boat with a more appealing reality passing her by. Possibly, one will pass close enough for her to make the death-defying leap to that boat, and hopefully to freedom. Used in this chapter, the term *transcendence* is exactly this—the departure of one's present reality in favor of another.

Figure 3-1

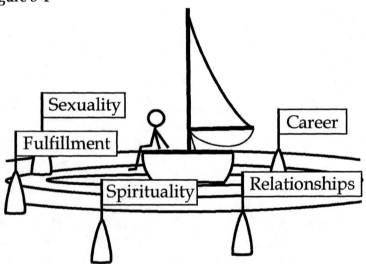

Alexis, like most Xers, is astute in her position. As we saw in the first chapter, the disillusionments and painful events of our unique upbringings, as well as today's intergenerational tensions, leave us with a healthy skepticism. Alexis is not easily satisfied with any one given project and she has made an important realization. Like a crab outgrowing its shell, she knows that she is trapped by her projects and that she cannot find satisfaction there.[2] In fact, to stay in her shell means to eventually suffocate. So, she is attempting to look for a way out. But it's a large, intimidating ocean, and Alexis shouldn't just carelessly abandon her cramped, but still-functioning, protective home.

What's out there anyway? Is there a better reality to be found in the supernatural? The hope is that there might be a cosmic reality to make life fuller, or more complete. Also using the analogy of the sailboat, one scholar, John Dominic Crossan, tells how he experiences life beyond the confines of his craft. Actually, he believes that it is impossible to leave one's boat. So instead, he says:

> One can sail *as close as possible* into the wind, and one can tell that you are as close as possible only by constantly testing the wind. Then the boat heels over, strains hard, and one experiences most fully, or at least I do, the thrill of sailing. My suggestion is that the excitement of transcendental experience is found only at the edge...and that the only way to find that excitement is to test those edges and those limits.[3]

In addition to this self-admission, a quick survey of Crossan's highly controversial theological endeavors indeed confirms that he very much tests "those edges and limits." Crossan's approach to truth, as well as his quest for the "historical Jesus," are viewed by many as unorthodox. Because Crossan intentionally pursues and pushes these edges and limits, we might say he is a theological adrenaline junkie. This is his pursuit of diversion.

What can we discern from all of this? The need of both Alexis and Crossan to pursue diversion demonstrates their dissatisfaction with the limits of life on their respective boats. Alexis is exploring the possibility of somehow moving off her boat. Crossan has explored this possibility and has determined it to be impossible. Instead, he finds transcendence by thrill-seeking at the limits of his boat. My contention is that although they are well intentioned, both Alexis and Crossan are pointed in the wrong direction.

As an Xer, Alexis is strategically positioned. She will not easily be fooled by the trappings of projects, and deeply desires to find more meaning in life. However, what she fails to realize is that pursuing a "better reality" in spirituality is also, in a very real sense, a project. It, like other projects, is a means through which she hopes to find an escape or diversion from her present reality — from her usual state of unhappiness. It is something that she is pursuing, even if for the sake of the pursuit alone. At least then she won't have time to contemplate the more serious, painful, and ever-present issues of life and death. Pascal speaks to Alexis' search for spirituality:

> However sad a man may be, if you can persuade him to take up some diversion he will be happy while it lasts, and however happy a man be, if he lacks diversion and has no absorbing passion or entertainment to keep boredom away, he will soon be depressed and unhappy.[4]

Without this diversion, observes Pascal, we are left to ponder what we really are.

In many instances, people do find diversion in the pursuit itself. The pursuit need not even have a specific goal. Pursuit for its own sake is how Crossan finds his "transcendental experience." Such pursuit can even be dangerous, especially because the adrenaline rush of the chase may become a normal escape project. Describing this effect in those who attempt to escape in cyberspace, philosopher Douglas Groothuis observes, "The thrill of driving a sports car for the first time might override our normal concerns for safety on the road....Speed may later become habitual."[5] Nothing more than a way to "give the finger" to death, such pursuit projects are also risky. They are risky because in pursuit, we tend to throw safety cautions to the wind. Even if we survive the ride, who knows exactly where we will land when our adrenaline high wears off?

Besides exposing ourselves to great risk, when spirituality is something that we seek, either as the object of our search or for the enjoyment of the chase alone, we again fall into the trappings of following a project. The project of spirituality is found in all spiritual endeavors and religions, including many approaches to Christianity. Pursuing spirituality is a way that we hope to escape the realities of our creatureness and it is therefore a project. The fact that a project is something "spiritual" in no way makes it any less of a project. Such pursuit, regardless of its objective, bears countless similarities to the projects that failed our parents. Instead of freeing us from bondage to our unpleasant reality, our search for transcendence actually becomes just another project bearing the opposite result of what we originally intended. Rather than freeing us, our quest for spirituality frustrates us and imprisons us in the same reality that we desire to deny.

I admit that I've been presenting a pretty bleak picture. We've seen that we are all inclined to live in denial of the fact that we are ultimately food for worms. Becker sums this up by saying that "the essence of normality is the refusal of reality."[6] So, in order to refuse reality, we intentionally and unintentionally pursue various projects. However, these projects simply encircle us, anesthetize us, and block us from truly escaping our reality. They serve no purpose other than to delay our face-to-face confrontation with our creaturely finitude until the day death knocks at our door. What's being implied here? Does the fact that we cannot avoid falling into projects mean that we are just robots or instinctive animals with no free will at all? We're back to our original question: What's the point? How can we get ourselves out of this bind? Our options have withered away. Even Becker observes that *all the psychological analysis in the world doesn't allow us to find out who we are, why we are here on earth, why we have to die, and how we can find victory.*[7] This said, we must now somehow find meaning in the midst of this apparent hopelessness.

Reflections

In what ways does society affirm this chapter's opening quotation by Blaise Pascal?

Can you think of ways you might "prefer the hunt to the capture" (see chapter's opening quote from Pascal)?

Why is "the supernatural" or "spirituality" a sexy escape from one's circle of projects?

How might religion simply be an easy way for people to hide from their reality (page 41)?

Chapter Four

Falling Upward

Satan and man, having fallen from God and been deserted by God, cannot will good, that is, things which please God or which God wills; but instead they are continually turned in the direction of their own desires, so that they are unable not to seek the things of self.[1]

— Martin Luther (1483-1546)

Adam and Eve

"You will surely not die," the serpent said to the woman. "For God knows that when you eat of it your eyes will be opened, and you will be like God, knowing good and evil."

When the woman saw that the fruit of the tree was good for food and pleasing to the eye, and also desirable for gaining wisdom, she took some and ate it. She also gave some to her husband, who was with her, and he ate it. Then, the eyes of both of them were opened, and they realized they were naked; so they sewed fig leaves together and made coverings for themselves. (Genesis 3:4-7)

This account about Adam and Eve, a common tradition in numerous different faiths, is not just about two people who lived ages ago. It's about all of humanity—including us. I say this because the parallels between their story and ours are uncanny. Adam and Eve were somehow dissatisfied with life as God's creatures in the garden. God gave them life in their own plot of paradise, and it was not enough for them. Instead, they ate from the tree of the knowledge of good and evil. Adam and Eve pursued an ideal of happiness that they expected would take them to greater heights than where they were placed by their creator in his goodness. As soon as they took this step, however, they became conscious and embarrassed of their created condition. So, they sewed fig leaves together and made coverings for themselves. Adam and Eve took action to deny their creatureness, and our projects are no different! Truly, this story is about us too!

Theologian Gerhard Forde rightly labels this rebellion the *upward fall*. It is our desire to transcend our created condition. God created Adam and Eve, placed them in the garden, and told them to tend it. The only stipulation God gave them was to not eat from the tree of the knowledge of good and evil. But, the serpent dangled a higher ideal in front of them, and in their quest for higher wisdom, they "crossed the line." They became concerned with God's realm *above* the concerns God had given them. They wanted to have control in God's realm over concerns that were God's. In effect, they rejected God's control over their lives and sought to become their own gods. We commonly refer to this as "the fall," but contrary to the natural imagery this term projects, Adam and Eve did not fall downward. The thought that they lost many of their created characteristics, subsequently falling down into a more evil state, is not the key. Rather, they misused their created characteristics. Although they were made in God's image, they refused to image God, or to reflect God's characteristics, by caring for the garden they were given. Their rebellion against God by moving from their created realm *below* into God's realm *above* marks their loss of faith and trust in their creator.[2] Their relationship with God was broken. This move into God's realm is the *upward* movement about which Forde speaks.

Our obsession with becoming gods above ourselves and the realm of creation for which God gave us to care is what Martin Luther calls *the bondage of the will.* Luther observes, "If we are under a god of this world, away from the work and Spirit of the true God, we are held captive to [the devil's] will (see II Tim. 2:26)...so that we cannot will anything but what he wills."[3] "Original sin itself, therefore, leaves free choice with no capacity to do anything but sin and be damned."[4] Even our most well-intentioned efforts to avoid bondage bind us. For example, our best attempts to do good in this world are often still done somewhat selfishly—because it feels good (self gratification) to do good, or because we hope to somehow earn "eternal points." Our motives cannot be completely pure and free. We are trapped.

The ramifications of the upward fall are quite evident to us as Xers in the projects of our surrounding society. Having been directly affected by the earthly consequences of these projects, we aren't quickly deceived by the serpent's suggestions of the American Dream and career satisfaction as ends in themselves. Such projects have frequently led to broken families, spoiled natural resources, and a gigantic national debt, and have left us quite unimpressed. As we noted in the last chapter with Alexis, such harsh realities leave us Xers in an astute position. If not consciously, we are at least unconsciously aware of the serpent's deceptive activity. We've been burned by our parents' chase after ideals and we now have a healthy skepticism, even apathy, toward both the ideals and the pursuit. So, we are tuned-in to the existence and dangers of projects. This seems to be the benefit of our healthy skepticism.

Ironically, though, the serpent uses our "healthy" skepticism to trick us. Because our endeavors don't resemble our parents' projects, we're feel that we're in the clear. But our healthy skepticism, rebellion, and apathy inevitably lead us back into our own projects. In our skepticism, we might cautiously look for "safe" alternative projects. In our rebellion, our projects are what oppose our elders. Or, in our apathy, we determine to take life as it unfolds before us and to not have projects—in which case our apathy becomes our project. In any case, we are attempting to replace God's control of our life with our own. This illusion of self-control indicates that we've already meddled in God's realm *above*. Our supposedly healthy skepticism boomerangs around and smacks us from behind. By thinking that our skepticism gives us more control by making us astute enough to avoid having a project and falling upward, the serpent has its way with us. We are simply engaging in an anti-project project, clamoring for control. The bottom line is that we are trapped in our projects. That's the "hell" of the whole thing.

Reflections

What action of Adam and Eve led to their "fall" (page 46)?

Explain the difference between God's realm *above* and humanity's realm *below* (pages 46-47).

Explain why the action of Adam and Eve was an attempt to replace God with themselves (pages 46-47).

How might you sometimes replace God's control over life with your own control?

Part 2

God's Reality

Chapter Five

Is God Relevant?

Sociologists long have known that radical social change and revolution do not occur because things are deplorable as much as they occur when people see the possibilities of what could be. Little tastes of the party God has in store for us make me want to destroy the unjust social arrangements in this world that keep the party called "God's Kingdom" from being realized.[1]

— Tony Campolo

You might have wondered why, starting with the previous chapter, I turned to God as a means to describe the predicament of our bondage to various projects. No matter where you stand in your views or understandings of God, I encourage you to continue reading, as I am confident that you will find at least some measure of relevance in the Christian tradition as it applies to the plight of Generation X. I say this because God *is* relevant. God is not just relevant for people seeking spirituality or answers to questions about life after death. As the above quote from Tony Campolo alludes, God is concretely relevant for our world and it's inhabitants — here and now. And Generation X is no exception! The basic tenets of Christianity relate to the realities facing our generation in a way

53

that is uncannily fitting for us. So, let's now take a look at a few of the many parallels between our GenX experience and the Christian experience.

First is that our concerns, hopes, and dreams for our own generation and future generations seem largely to fall on deaf ears. Many of those who control our society refuse to take us seriously. Our input has little or no value. Jesus experienced this frustration too. He was the bearer of good news about God's healing love, forgiveness, and reconciliation. Jesus had vision and was genuinely concerned for people and their future. Yet, not only did his contemporaries turn a deaf ear, but they mocked him, tortured him, and eventually executed him. Jesus can definitely relate to our frustrations in this area!

Second, we know about pain. Because we have been buried by fallout from the escapades of our project-pursuing elders, we are deeply aware that our world and the people in it are far from perfect. We are keenly aware of the existence of injustice. Similarly, Christianity also suggests that our world is imperfect. In fact, our broken world and people's bondage to self-serving projects are foundational to everything about Christianity. The entire biblical history of God's interaction with our world revolves around its imperfection.

Third, we value meaningful relationships. Many of us were cheated out of some of our most primary relationships in life. Many of our elders have modeled relationships of convenience—both in their personal and professional realms. This hasn't given us a strong example to follow, but it has dramatically reinforced the importance of "real" relationships to us. Although many aspects of our future may be uncertain, we will always have each other. God also values relationships. God advocates that we maintain strong, meaningful relationships with other people, as well as with God. Jesus, God's Son, modeled this well. He resonated with people interested in being real and vulnerable—not with those who thought they were perfect and had life by the tail. Jesus accepted people as they really were, with all their imperfections. Jesus preferred that people not erect facades.

Figure 5-1

Parallels

GenX	Christianity
We feel discounted by those in control.	Jesus was not taken seriously and was eventually mocked, tortured, and executed.
We've obviously inherited a terribly imperfect world.	Our imperfect world is foundational to Christian understanding.
We want relationships with depth and meaning.	Jesus sought "real" relationships, accepting people as they were.
We are tired of prejudice and injustice against us and others.	Jesus reached out to the unacceptable and desired equality for all.

A fourth parallel relates to prejudice. We are sick and tired of the problems in this world unnecessarily caused by racial, cultural, social, and generational prejudices. People are people! Our sentiment is timely, as our population in America is rapidly becoming more blended. God loves us all equally, regardless of our situation in life. In fact, God hopes for reconciliation! Jesus intentionally reached out to the underdogs. If someone was the wrong race, was politically incorrect, was too old or too young, spoke the wrong language, worshipped in the wrong church, worked in an unacceptable profession, or suffered from a "sinful" disease, Jesus intentionally sought and reached out to them. God wants a level playing field and equality for all people. God wants us to live in true community.

These above parallels between GenX and Christianity are just a few of many, and they speak well of the relevance of God for us as a generation. But God's relevance for us is also much more personal!

My own experience speaks to this personal relevance. In my early twenties, I began to ask questions like, "Why have I chosen my current career path? What are my strategic goals in life? How do these goals match what I understand to be my purpose in life? What is my purpose in life, anyway?" These questions and others like them thrusted me into deep reflection about my life and its purpose, and of course, about God. After some intense soul-searching and prayer, I realized that my situation in life had resulted from me pursuing my own project of becoming a pilot. I had failed to include God in my planning. While my chosen career of being an Air Force pilot is good for many, it was not where God wanted me to use my gifts.

My decision to leave the career I had pursued since I was three years old turned my life upside-down. I didn't know at the time where it was God wanted me to be, but I knew it was not flying. After some time had passed and I had grieved over the loss of my dream, I began to experience a new sense of peace that I had never before experienced. I didn't realize at the time that the reason for this was that I had surrendered a large portion of control over my destiny. God was working in my life, and I was listening. I had dropped my biggest project aimed at being my own god. As I listened more to God and lifted-up my own goals less, I realized that God was carrying me toward his goals. And God's goals were awesome—much better than I could have ever devised for myself.

I had recently married another Air Force officer. After

much prayer and soul searching, we both agreed that we would leave the Air Force so I could attend seminary. Right after we finalized our irreversible decisions to leave our careers with the Air Force, we were surprised to learn my wife was pregnant and due that fall—in the middle of my first quarter of school! Because we had just finished paying-off our debt and had not accumulated any savings, we had planned on her getting a full-time job to pay our living expenses and my school bills. As obstacles in our future began to seem insurmountable, this was a very anxious time for us! However, the more we lived with the situation, the more we realized that our well being was in God's hands, and our sense of peace grew. Our journey has not, and is still not, always easy. But knowing that we are where God wants us to be gives us peace that passes all understanding. God is relevant!

Our God, the master peacemaker in our lives, is relevant. God meets each of us right where we are in life and breaks us free from the bonds of our projects so that we may follow him. God does this freely for us, demanding nothing in return. I don't know where God's plan will take me ten years from now. But I do know that regardless of what my situation in life will be, and in spite of the fact that I will continue to struggle against my own desire to grab the reigns of control, under God's direction I will have a God-given sense of peace.

Does God have a plan for your life? Absolutely! It is the best plan possible for you. Even in times when you doubt his relevance, God is there for you. And in times when you are open to God's will, you will realize his relevance in your life, and you will find peace that passes all understanding.

In this second part of the book, we will explore more about God and his relevance for us. We will look more closely at how God has related, and continues to relate, to us. We will see how, out of love for us, God frees us from bondage to our own god-projects and recreates us as his children. We will explore key aspects of our new relationship with our creator. And we will enjoy some illustrations that help hit-home our role vs. God's role in this relationship.

Reflections

What about your past understanding of God is negative?

What about your past understanding of God is positive?

Do you have any goals that you're not willing to give-up, even for God?

Why might releasing control over your destiny give you peace (pages 56-57)?

What does it mean to be open to God's will (pages 56-57)?

In this chapter's opening quotation, Campolo refers to the "possibilities of what could be." What possibilities for life do you envision?

Chapter Six

The Accident

> A child is playing in the street. A truck is bearing down on the child. A man casts himself in the path of the truck, saves the child, but is himself killed in the process. It is an accident.[1]
>
> —*Gerhard Forde*

The serpent has had its way with us. Even our best efforts to escape our created condition result in circular, endless projects. We are in bondage to sin and cannot free ourselves. If these statements are all we can say, then the devil has won. As we will see, though, God has acted and has defeated the devil.

Forde uses an ingenious twist in the above accident scenario to illustrate just how it is that God breaks us out of bondage. The event directly impacts three people: the truck driver, the child, and the man who is killed. Let's first look at the man who gave his life. This man's death is clearly a sacrifice. It is not a sacrifice *to* anyone or anything. He did not give his life in order to appease or make payment to the driver of the truck or the child, or even some type of god. Rather, he gave his life *for* the child. This is the same way that we describe the heroic death of soldiers in battle. Such soldiers sacrifice their life *for* their country. We do not speak as if their lives were sacrifices *to* something. When we recognize that the man in this illustration is Jesus, it is enough for us to say that Jesus sacrificed his life *for us*.

But are we the relatively innocent child who made the mistake of playing on the street? Forde argues that we are more properly placed behind the wheel of the truck. There we are, driving our Mack truck through life—maybe just a few miles per hour over the speed limit through a residential neighborhood in which we have no business—and in Forde's words, "suddenly there is someone who throws himself in our unheeding way and is splattered against the front of our machine."[2] The hard part to stomach here is that we did it. We killed Jesus. After all, without our deadly driving, he would not have needed to sacrifice himself. As we have seen, our bondage to sin causes us to refuse to stay out of the driver's seat (our conglomeration of projects), and we can't avoid the temptation to take shortcuts through residential neighborhoods (God's realm *above*). In effect, we have said "No" to God, who subsequently responded with a "Yes!" The end result is that in the sacrifice of Jesus, God has saved us from ourselves.

It is not enough to only look at Jesus' sacrifice for us. To stop there is to stop short of hope beyond this life. Jesus is dead and we killed him—end of story. But we must also look to the resurrection. It is the resurrection following the sacrifice that ultimately turns death into life and defeat into victory. Forde says it well; "The one splattered against the front of our truck comes back to say 'Shalom' (peace)...The one we killed, the one no one wanted, is raised from the dead."[3] "He broke through the closed circle and brought new light in his resurrection. Without the resurrection, the cross has no importance for us."[4]

Jesus is the way out of our bondage within our circle of projects. To cognitively know this is not enough. We must actually go through the cross and resurrection.[5] This is possible because Jesus has so closely identified with us that his death becomes our death—his resurrection becomes our resurrection.[6] He has died ahead of us, bringing death to us. The news of Jesus' death and resurrection must kill us and make us alive again. It is God who kills us and gives us new life when we hear these words of good news. This is something that *God* does to us. To approach this as something that *we* do is to fall into the trap of making the whole thing into a project.

Experiencing death and resurrection in our lives means that God yanks us out of the driver's seat and gives us a new lease on life. This happens when we hear the words of good news—when Jesus returns to us with words of peace and forgiveness. *God is no longer our project—we are God's project.* Our contemporary quests for transcendence are overshadowed by the Transcendent. God recreates us, freeing us as his creation to love and trust him and nothing more.[7] As God's children, we finally become the down-to-earth people that God always hoped we would be. But we should not be so naive to think that we instantly become perfect creatures. Even as a new creation, we still live in tension with the "old Adam" — our old selves that want to remain in the driver's seat. Forde explains that "we are not yet one with Christ completely. In this life the old Adam is still with us and is all too much alive."[8] To deal with this, we return to the cross daily: "Our sinful self, with all its evil deeds and desires, should be drowned through daily repentance; and day after day a new self should arise to live in God with righteousness and purity forever."[9]

Returning to the cross daily means that in spite of the many tensions in which we live, God, through word of Jesus' sacrifice and resurrection, kills us and resurrects us daily (more on this in the next chapter). This allows us to live in a continually renewed relationship with our creator. We have a new appreciation for what it means to be a creature! Rather then obsessing about how to take control of our lives, we look around and find ourselves in the garden with a newfound freedom to take care of the world God has given us. Our hope is not that we, under our own initiative, might fix this world or escape from it. Rather, our hope is in God's plan of reconciliation and recovery for our world. Today, this has enormous implications for the natural environment and our relationships with our neighbors—both next-door and around the world—that we Xers have inherited. This gives a whole new meaning to R.E.M.'s lyrics, "It's the end of the world as we know it"!

Reflections

What is the difference between a sacrifice *to* something and a sacrifice *for* something (pages 61-62)?

How is delving into God's realm above saying "No" to God (page 62)?

How is it that we killed Jesus by delving into God's realm above (page 62)?

Why is it important that we look not only to Jesus' sacrifice, but also to his resurrection (page 62)?

What might it mean to be God's project instead of making God your own project (pages 62-63)?

How does Jesus' sacrifice and resurrection free you to engage the world around you (pages 63-64)?

Chapter Seven

The Offense

> *Regarding Jesus:*   Humanly speaking, what an insane misrelationship: between an individual human being who will not even let himself be helped — and — him! No human being could endure this misrelationship; only the God-man can do that.[1]
>
> — *Soren Kierkegaard (1813-1855)*

We have seen that to give us a new life free from bondage to sin, it is necessary that Jesus first kill us. Exactly how does Jesus do this? He does this by offending our old, project-pursuing selves right into the grave. Kierkegaard says that Jesus offends by being both God and human. Separately, they are not offensive. We expect God to act like God and people to act like people. But for God to be a person is too much for us to grasp. For God to pursue and relate to us as one of us eliminates our need to pursue God and thus threatens our projects to be like God.[2]

Let's take a quick survey of Jesus' life. From the view of most of Jesus' contemporaries, his birth was illegitimate. Mary, Jesus' birth mother, was unwed. Joseph, Mary's fiancé, initially resolved to quietly break off their relationship. After the revelation of the virginal conception from a heavenly messenger, Joseph did end up marrying Mary. The result is that Jesus grew-up in a blended family from a disliked town called Nazareth. He took a long time to decide on a career, as he was in his early thirties before he began his public ministry. By cultural standards, his career path was a poor choice. He chose to work outside the established Jewish religious institution. In many ways, he even opposed the institution. He was an advocate for the poor and oppressed, and he didn't bother with "fake" people. Jesus was very involved in serving his surrounding community, and he valued the relationships he developed. He knew a good party when he saw one. He even turned water into wine to keep a wedding reception going. Given all these characteristics, it's as if Jesus was an Xer in his own time![3]

The offense is in the fact that Jesus was the most human person ever. He was the perfect human creature. He identified with us (not just Xers, but all generations) in all aspects. His body's physiology was just like ours—completely human. He cried. He entered into relationships with other people. He felt anger and compassion. He lived, and he even died. Contrary to the rest of humanity, though, he had not fallen into sin (a corrupted relationship with God) with the rest of us. He enjoyed a perfect relationship with God the Father. Jesus had no use for projects to deny his creatureness and to be like God. God was being the perfect human for us, yet we were trying like mad to escape our created relationship with God and to become more like him. God came down to meet us on our own level, but we wouldn't have him—we were on our way up.

We refused to let God be God. Our projects became our gods. Luther observes, "That to which your heart clings and entrusts itself is, I say, really your God."[4] Because there is only one true God, our "god-projects," our efforts to replace God in our own lives, can only conflict with God and thus be threatened by God. Because in the fall we are all bound to our projects, Jesus could only be rejected by both his contemporaries and by us. Kierkegaard says this well:

> When an individual appeals to his relationship with God over against the established order that has deified itself, it does indeed seem as if he were making himself more than human....The established order wants to be a totality that recognizes nothing above itself but has every individual under it and judges every individual who subordinates himself to the established order. But the single individual who teaches the most humble and yet also the most human doctrine about what it means to be a human being, the established order will intimidate with charging him with being guilty of blasphemy.[5]

To find true humanity is to eliminate the need for our god-projects. It is Jesus' perfect, projectless humanity that testifies to his divinity—only God could be so human. One biblical description of Jesus especially emphasizes this:

> Who being in very nature God, did not consider equality with God something to be grasped, but made himself nothing, taking the very nature of a servant, being made in human likeness. And being found in appearance as a man, he humbled himself and became obedient to death—even death on a cross! (Philippians 2:6-8)

As author Henri Nouwen observes, "God became a little baby. Who can be afraid of a little baby? A tiny little baby is completely dependent."[6] In Jesus of Nazareth, the 'powerless' God appeared among us to unmask our illusions of power and control[7]—"telling us that not to be in control is part of the human condition."[8] In this willingness to be fully human, Jesus "does God to us"[9] and thus threatens our god-projects. Our instinctive defense almost 2,000 years ago was to kill him, and our reaction today is no different.

Jesus identifies with us closer than we want. The result is like our reaction to step back or push away when someone invades our personal space. In today's world that advocates individual rights and freedom, we are taught that our space is our own. We are quick to claim our rights to choose our relationships and to determine who can meddle in our space—even if the meddler is God. Only faith—trusting God over ourselves—can remove the offense of God's identification with us. It is in faith that we regain our proper relationship with God and thus our humanity.

Reflections

In what ways was Jesus fully human (page 68)?

Why are we threatened by the fact that God became human (page 68-70)?

Why does perfect humanity entail being without god-projects (page 69)?

Explain this statement: "God came down to meet us on our own level, but we wouldn't have him—we were on our way up" (page 68).

Was our rejection of Jesus inevitable (page 69)? Why or why not?

Consider some ways that you might feel threatened by Jesus (think of how Jesus might threaten some of your own projects).

What allows us to remove the offense of God's identification with us (page 70)?

Chapter Eight

Faith and Grace

Every faculty you have, your power of thinking of moving your limbs from moment to moment, is given you by God. It is like a small child going to his father and saying, "Daddy, give me a sixpence to buy you a birthday present." Of course, the father does, and he is pleased with the child's present. It is all nice and proper, but only an idiot would think that the father is sixpence to the good on the transaction.[1]

—*C. S. Lewis (1898-1963)*

It may seem strange that I have entitled this chapter with two terms that are commonly treated separately. However, it is my contention that these terms are too closely related to effectively treat them apart from one another—having faith requires God's grace. Let's begin by looking at two Bible passages that are central to understanding faith and grace.

First, "For God so loved the world that he gave his one and only Son, that whoever believes in him shall not perish but have eternal life" (John 3:16).

Second, "For it is by grace you have been saved, through faith—and this not from yourselves, it is the gift of God—not by works, so that no one can boast" (Ephesians 2:8-9).

Combined, these two passages give us a confession something like:

> We cannot obtain forgiveness of sin and righteousness before God by our own merits, works, or satisfactions, but that we receive forgiveness of sin and become righteous before God by grace, for Christ's sake, through faith, when we believe that Christ suffered for us and that for his sake our sin is forgiven and righteousness and eternal life are given to us.[2]

If we only look at the first passage, John 3:16, we don't see the entire picture. Because it says, "whoever believes in him shall not perish," we assume that we are to take the action of believing (the same word in the original Greek language is used for both believing and having faith). However, the language here is not *prescribing* an action that we are to undertake. We are not being told that we'd better go now and believe if we don't want to perish. This passage is *describing* the condition of one who does not perish. It does not tell us what the source of our belief is. It just tells us that we must have it. Faith is best understood as our relationship with God itself.[3] *Faith is our state of being grasped by God's promise of salvation.* It is trusting God over ourselves. As with a man and a woman who have fallen in love, yielding such control to the other is not a "having to," it's a "wanting to."[4]

This becomes clearer when we move to the next passage, Ephesians 2:8-9. This passage ties faith directly to God's grace. We are told explicitly that it is *by grace* we have been saved through faith, and that this reality is the gift of God. The statement "it is the gift of God" is preceded by the statement, "this is not of yourselves," and followed by the statement, "not by works, so that no one can boast." Here are three back-to-back statements emphasizing God's action and eliminating ours. *To think that something within our human capacity can right our relationship with God is nothing less than to turn salvation into our own project.* Of course, this would be a dead end. Salvation is God's business.

Our need for grace is illustrated by a broken marriage relationship. Can the relationship be fixed by having either partner seek fulfillment in intimate extramarital relationships? Not at all! Yet, our insistence on pursuing our own projects and seeking fulfillment apart from our relationship with our Creator is no different. Our search for fulfillment in careers, money, extreme sports, sexuality, good deeds, pessimism, a resolve to avoid projects, or any other project, is adulterous to our relationship with God. And the ugly truth is that we've all done it. We've all been adulterous before God in some way. *Only unconditional forgiveness can restore our relationship with God.* Fortunately, in amazing grace, God's forgiveness flows freely. Such grace generates great faith in us![5]

God's grace is saturating. It is not only the forerunner of faith, but also the result (see Romans 5:2). This fact, along with what we have found by examining the passages above, demonstrates that faith and grace are inseparable. They come as a package. To use an oversimplified analogy, faith and grace are like a wind and a sailboat. Let's first look at grace. Referring to the entire cosmos, the Apostle Paul tells us that Jesus Christ is "before all things, and in him all things hold together" (Colossians 1:17). Because our lives on this earth are part of the cosmos, we can say that whether we realize it or not, Jesus also holds our lives together in his grace. We'll call each of our individual grace-filled lives a sailboat. Now let's look at faith. Viewing faith as a wind, it is faith that keeps us from drifting aimlessly. In the same way that God gives us the wind, God gives us faith. It fills the sails of our sailboat, pushing us forward through the waves. Our properly operating sailboat is both grace-filled and faith-powered. Paul describes this well;

"Before this faith came, we were held prisoners by the law, locked up until faith should be revealed" (Galatians 3:23).

Because faith is the necessary condition of salvation, and because we are incapable of having faith by any action of our own (as we are incapable of commanding the wind), we can say that our salvation is given to us. In other words, as God gives us the wind, God also gives us faith and thus salvation. Both the wind and faith cost us nothing—they are free. And although we are trapped by our projects and cannot free ourselves, God, who *is* free, does it for us by giving us faith. What a gift! Paul clearly explains this in his letter to the Christians in Rome, "For all have sinned and fall short of the glory of God, and all are justified freely by his grace through the redemption that came by Christ Jesus" (Romans 3:23-24).

As we have already noted, though, we are inclined to reject God's forgiving grace—even though God gives it to us freely. We are drawn towards projects to deny or abandon the sailboats (grace-filled lives) God has given us. We are not content to be drifting in the sea, but we are not patient enough to wait for a good, strong wind (faith) either. Rather, we decide that if we are to make any headway, we must take matters into our own hands. We try to flee our situation by fleeing our sailboat, or at least by trying to generate our own wind—a futile endeavor. If God gave us a sailboat, he will also give us wind! But even when God does fill our sails with a little wind, we are not always content. The wind causes our sailboat to heel over slightly and we begin to inch forward. The significance of God's grace then becomes evident to us and we panic. In our uncertainty, we still try to flee from God's grace and thus from God himself. God-given grace and faith are so contrary to our paradigms in life that they can only scare us away. Luther has a great personal story illustrating this point:

It's very difficult for a man to believe that God is

gracious to him. The human heart can't grasp this. This is the way we are....Christ offers himself to us together with the forgiveness of sins, yet we flee from his face.

This also happened to me as a boy in my homeland when we sang in order to gather sausages. A townsman jokingly cried out, "what are you boys up to? May this or that evil overtake you!" At the same time, he ran toward us with two sausages. With my companion I took to my feet and ran away from the man who was offering his gift. This is precisely what happens to us in our relation to God. He gave us Christ with all his gifts, and yet we flee from him and regard him as our judge.[6]

Luther has it right. When God offers us the gift, our instinct is to flee.

A solid understanding of faith and grace is central to our grasp of God's intended reality for us. But, at the same time, it is extremely difficult for us to absorb this understanding. So, the next two chapters contain illustrations to "hit-home" what God's spectacular gifts of faith and grace mean for us.

Reflections

How is our faith in God like the love expressed within the romantic relationship of two people (page 74)?

How is our own pursuit of fulfillment the opposite of faith (page 75)?

Why is God's forgiveness necessary for us to have relationship-restoring faith in God (page 75)?

How is our faith in God similar to the present given by the child in the opening quotation by C.S. Lewis?

Why is God's gift of unconditionally free grace so hard for us to stomach (pages 76-77)?

Chapter Nine

Three Parables

> Infants who have no works are saved by faith alone, and therefore faith alone justifies. If the power of God can do this in one person it can do it in all, because it's not the power (or the weakness) of the infant but the power of faith.[1]
> —*Martin Luther (1483-1546)*

In this chapter, we will look at three of Jesus' parables that help our understanding of how, in grace, God gives us faith and rescues us from our due. All from the fifteenth chapter of Luke, they are the parables of The Lost Sheep, The Lost Coin, and The Lost Son.[2]

The Parable of the Lost Sheep (Luke 15:3-7)

Suppose one of you has a hundred sheep and loses one of them. Does he not leave the ninety-nine in the open country and go after the lost sheep until he finds it? And when he finds it, he joyfully puts it on his shoulders and goes home. Then he calls his friends and neighbors together and says, "Rejoice with me; I have found my lost sheep." I tell you that in the same way there is more rejoicing in heaven over one sinner who repents than over ninety-nine righteous persons who do not need to repent.

Does this parable hit home? Here we are...sheep who have strayed away. If anything, our actions hamper our safety and salvation. Yet, God has intently tracked you down, found you, and carried you to the safety of his care. And there is rejoicing in heaven!

The Parable of the Lost Coin (Luke 15:8-10)

Or suppose a woman has ten silver coins and loses one. Does she not light a lamp, sweep the house and search carefully until she finds it? And when she finds it, she calls her friends and neighbors together and says, "Rejoice with me; I have found my lost coin." In the same way, I tell you, there is rejoicing in the presence of the angels of God over one sinner who repents.

Here we are again...this time lost coins. A lost coin can do nothing to return itself to its rightful owner. In fact, many other people, upon finding a loose coin, would snatch it up and keep it. But knowing you were lost, God has carefully searched for you, found you, and reclaimed you into his care. And there is rejoicing in heaven!

The Parable of the Lost Son (Luke 15:11-31)

There was a man who had two sons. The younger one

said to his father, "Father, give me my share of the estate." So he divided his property between them.

Not long after that, the younger son got together all he had, set off for a distant country and there squandered his wealth in wild living. After he had spent everything, there was a severe famine in that whole country, and he began to be in need. So, he went and hired himself out to a citizen of that country, who sent him to his fields to feed his pigs. He longed to fill his stomach with the pods that the pigs were eating, but no one gave him anything.

When he came to his senses, he said, "How many of my father's hired men have food to spare, and here I am starving to death! I will set out and go back to my father and say to him: Father, I have sinned against heaven and against you. I am no longer worthy to be called your son; make me like one of your hired men." So he got up and went to his father. But while he was still a long way off, his father saw him and was filled with compassion for him; he ran to his son, threw his arms around him and kissed him.

The son said to him, "Father, I have sinned against heaven and against you. I am no longer worthy to be called your son.

But the father said to his servants, "Quick! Bring the best robe and put it on him. Put a ring on his finger and sandals on his feet. Bring the fattened calf and kill it. Let's have a feast and celebrate. For this son of mine was dead and is alive again; he was lost and is found." So they began to celebrate. (Verses 25-31 omitted).

In this parable, the son recognizes his sin and resolves to tell his father. Yet, before he has a chance to repent, his father runs to him and embraces him. It is only after the father embraces his son that the son repents.

Here we are again…this time lost children of God. Before you had a chance to repent, God saw your predicament, was filled with compassion, ran to you, and has thrown his arms around you. The celebration has begun!

What do these three parables hit home to us? They remind us that although you were lost, God deeply valued you and cared for you so much that he intentionally pursued you. God found you and returned you to the safety of his loving care. For this, God rejoices and celebrates. God is overjoyed with your return! You were saved because you were loved by your savior.

Faith is recognizing God's saving action in our lives. As we have said before, *faith is the state of being grasped by God's promise of salvation.* What does God say to you as he embraces you and returns you to his care and away from your certain destruction? God says, "It is I, don't be afraid. Your faith has healed you. You are mine. I love you. I forgive your sins." And what did you have to do? *Absolutely Nothing.* For it is by grace you have been saved through faith—and this not from yourselves, it is the gift of God. (Ephesians 2:8).

Reflections

How might you be like the lost sheep or the lost son?

Suppose the lost coin is you. Who or what in the world (verses God) would like to snatch you up and keep you?

In what ways has God pursued you (page 82)?

In what ways are you tempted to think that some action of yours must precede God's action in your life (page 82)?

What feelings do you have when you ponder the fact that God saved you even though you were unable to assist in your own salvation?

Chapter Ten

Naaman

> The good news differs from the law in that it does not link righteousness to works but lodges it solely in God's mercy.[1]
> —*John Calvin (1509-1564)*

The following illustration comes from II Kings 5:1-16—a passage in the Old Testament portion of our Bible that was written well before the birth of Jesus. Although it might be easy to view the Old Testament as a bunch of irrelevant, ancient rules and regulations, it is also full of God's promises and grace! Please note that what follows is my own commentary on the passage. There is nothing like going to the actual passage yourself, which of course, I highly recommend!

We are a self-centered nation. Our position in the world may be nearing its end, but at least at this point, we are still the most powerful nation in the world. A few years ago, our astronomical military budget finally forced the Soviet Union, by far our most significant military threat, into bankruptcy. The USSR has since broken-up, and we are now a superpower in a class by ourselves. Two realms of power exist in today's world—the military realm and the economic realm. No other nation rivals the United States' combination of military and economic might. Should Japan or an oil producing alliance like OPEC become upset with us, they might be able to impact us with some sort of economic embargo, but, we would survive. And, we always have the "big stick" of our military strength to help us get our way. China may be the closest nation to us in military strength, but they are increasingly reliant on our economic trade with them. Yes, we have it all—military and economic strength. This is why we are easily a self-centered nation.

So, for the most part, we can get what we want, wherever we want. Most nations want to be on our "preferred list." They will make concessions just to gain our favor. A prime example of this is the Persian Gulf war. My guess is that given a choice, most Middle-East nations would prefer to remain autonomous. Nevertheless, the Middle-East nations that hold the upper hand in the region are allied with the United States. They have made some concessions for the sake of stability. Kuwait's deliverance in the Gulf War is a prime example of this. We stopped the unjust invasion by Iraq's Saddam Hussain, and in return, we are able to retain a solid, relatively cheap, source of oil from Kuwait. Our motives may have included humanitarian concerns, but our primary concerns in the war were our economic and political interests. In other words, our motives stemmed from our self-centeredness.

American tourists also reflect this self-centeredness! If you've ever lived or traveled in Europe, you've probably seen the "ugly American tourist" who expects all the locals to speak English, and then gets frustrated when they don't. These Americans also expect to be served as if they were traveling in the U.S. They expect their Visa card to be accepted as an international currency, and are upset when it isn't. They want their beer cold, their soda with ice, and their menus in English.

They complain when their hotel room doesn't come with a shower. When body odor abounds because the locals don't wear deodorant, these Americans get incensed. And when they have to pay to use the toilet, they get pissed. But, the people of these countries often put up with the hassles of serving insensitive Americans because they want the Americans' money. In the meantime, Americans are earning America a bad name.

On the flip side, when foreigners visit America, we usually expect them to speak English, and get frustrated when they don't. This is changing in a few places, but even in places where it is, the change is slow. Life revolves around us! We expect the world to cater to us. I'd bet that we're the most self-centered nation on the planet. The sad thing is, I think that I might be one of these ugly Americans! Yes, I have traveled overseas and experienced my fair share of frustrations with local customs. And I too expect my Visa card to be taken wherever I go. Even in my hometown, I have been frustrated when calling in orders for Chinese take-out and not being able to speak in English to the people taking my order. Yes, much too often, I am an insensitive, self-centered, American.

Interestingly, there is a self-centered person in the Old Testament. His name is Naaman, and he's from Syria. In many ways, Syria was the America of its day. In fact, we are told that the Lord had recently given Naaman, the commander of the Syrian army, military victory over Israel. Naaman has a lot of things going for him. His army is powerful. He's a great man in the sight of his master, the King, and highly regarded. His master is also loaded with money. Naaman has a good life. He has no worries, except for one thing—he has leprosy. Having leprosy is an obvious concern for Naaman, because the tradition of Naaman's day equates having leprosy directly with being sinful. People would equate Naaman's leprosy with sin either in his life or in his family's. Despite his comfortable lifestyle and professional successes, this is a huge black mark in Naaman's life.

Fortunately for Naaman, an Israelite slave-girl suggests that Naaman see a prophet in Samaria to be cured from his leprosy. Naaman goes to his king, who supports Naaman fully, to request leave to travel to Samaria in order that he might be cured. Assuming that the power to heal Naaman is held by the King of Israel, Naaman's own king sends Naaman off to see the King of Israel, with an official letter and about a quarter of a million dollars—a doctor fee not unlike one we might encounter today! Unfortunately for Naaman, when he arrives in Israel, the king is unable to heal him. Probably in great fear, since Naaman's army had recently defeated Israel in battle, the King of Israel says something like, "who does your king think that I am, God? Can I kill and bring back to life? I don't have the power to do this!" And then the King of Israel tears his robes in distress.

God's prophet Elisha hears of the King of Israel's predicament and sends for Naaman. Naaman arrives at Elisha's house with his horses, his chariots, and his quarter of a million dollars. But, Elisha does not come out of his house to meet Naaman. Instead, he sends a messenger out to say to Naaman, "Go, wash yourself in the Jordan, and your flesh will be restored, and you will be cleansed."

Now, imagine General Colin Powell, the commander of the Allied Forces in the Gulf War, going to Iraq to undergo difficult surgery from a specially trained surgeon who happened to practice there. Shouldn't General Powell expect a little pomp and circumstance because of his importance? Shouldn't he also expect that the doctor would meet with him personally before the surgery? You would think so! And Naaman thinks so too. Elisha didn't, though, and Naaman is ticked! Here's what happens:

> But Naaman went away angry and said, "I
> thought that he would surely come out to me and stand
> and call on the name of the LORD his God, wave his
> hand over the spot and cure me of my leprosy. Are not
> Abana and Pharpar, the rivers of Damascus, better than
> any of the waters of Israel? Couldn't I wash in them and
> be cleansed?" So he turned and went off in a rage. (2
> Kings 5:11-12)

Elisha prescribes no bells and whistles. There is no formal
healing ceremony. Instead, Elisha tells Naaman, through a
messenger, to bathe in a river—something Naaman could have
done at home! Can you imagine the doctor in Iraq telling
General Powell, through an assistant, to go jump into the
Persian Gulf, and that he would then be cured? Naaman thinks
that he deserves more ceremony and personal attention than he
gets, so he stomps off in a rage.

In his self-centeredness, Naaman doesn't "get it."
Fortunately for him, though, his servants are more astute than
he is. Using some simple logic, they convince Naaman to give
Elisha's prescription a try. So, Naaman immerses himself in the
Jordan seven times and is cured of his leprosy. Naaman has
finally heard the Word of God, and he is cured. If we stop here,
we might think that this is the whole story. Sure, it's true that
the Word of God heals us, and that's Good News, but we need
to read the next two verses:

> Then Naaman and all his attendants went back to
> the man of God. He stood before him and said, "Now I
> know that there is no God in all the world except in
> Israel. Please accept now a gift from your servant."
> The prophet answered, "As surely as the LORD
> lives, whom I serve, I will not accept a thing." And even

though Naaman urged him, he refused. (2 Kings 5:15-16)

In verse eight, Elisha stated that his purpose for sending for Naaman was so that Naaman would know there is a prophet in Israel. If we ignored verses fifteen and sixteen, Elisha's purpose would be overshadowed by the fact that God has the power to heal. Instead, in verse fifteen, Naaman states, "Now I know that there is no God in all the world except in Israel." Elisha's purpose is now realized. Although God does heal in this story, the point here is not that God has the power to heal Naaman (although he certainly does). Rather, the point is that God acts in Naaman's life in order for him to have faith.

But there is more! Naaman still doesn't get the big picture. At the end of verse fifteen, he's ready to pay his doctor's bill. A quarter of a million dollars is a small price to pay to get rid of leprosy and the sinful social stigma attached to it—especially for an important man like Naaman. And for a man of integrity like Naaman, it only seems fair to him that he pay for Elisha's services. But we find in verse sixteen that Elisha refuses to accept any payment from Naaman. After all, it was God who truly healed Naaman.

Here is Naaman, an important man. He thinks he's in control of his life. He is buddies with his king. He has a ton of money. But none of that matters to God. Despite Naaman's self-centeredness, God breaks through to Naaman and heals him. And what does God require from Naaman in return? *Absolutely Nothing*.

Here we are. Although most of us do not hold power-positions like Naaman, I wonder if there's not a little of Naaman in each of us. We live in the most powerful nation in the world. Compared to most people in the world, our lives as Xers are easy—we have many comforts. Sure, we've faced our share of trials and tribulations, and we face a tenuous future. But like

Naaman, we desperately want to maintain control of our lives. We each want to be our own god. Our self-centeredness makes us want to participate in our healing and salvation. Naaman desperately wanted to pay for his healing. His pride was at stake if he just accepted a handout! This would be embarrassing! But, it is impossible to pay-off God with our money, our influence, our good deeds, or anything that we can do. All the money in the world and all the actions we can perform cannot fill our sails with a saving faith! *God does not need anything from us. We need God.* Elisha would have nothing to do with Naaman's offer to pay for his healing. Like Naaman, it's this free gift that's so hard for us to comprehend.

In the same way that God healed Naaman, God has healed you. Christ died and was resurrected for you. God has given you eternal life by sacrificing his Son for you. And what does God expect from you in return? *Absolutely Nothing*—It's God's gift to you!

Reflections

In what ways does our society promote the value of an independent or self-centered attitude?

Naaman initially seeks help in the wrong place (page 88). How might we sometimes make the same mistake?

How can our pride interfere with our relationship with God (pages 88-91)?

In what ways do we sometimes try to "pay-off" God (pages 90-91)?

How does it feel to realize that God will not accept any payment you can give for your salvation, and that God saves you nevertheless?

Part 3

Living in Reality

Chapter Eleven

Bad Stuff

> To think of God apart from Jesus Christ strikes terror in our hearts because we see a God whom we blame for all adversity, chaos, destruction, and punishment.[1]
>
> — *Wayne Oates*

But what good is all this free grace and faith talk in the face of all the bad stuff that happens in the world? This is a critical question. It is a dangerous question to address because it places me on the threshold of trying to explain what God has reserved for his realm *above*. In other words, addressing the existence of evil in our world is an attempt to address something that God has not fully revealed to us—the details remain hidden. The existence of evil in our world is a subject pondered by theologians from around the world. Our wondering about why we must endure pain will continue with no definite resolution until we are before God's throne and can ask him personally! Attempting to describe partially or completely hidden aspects of God or God's plan is to engage in our own god-projects. Of course, much of this book does the same thing! However, because this question about God (why bad stuff happens) seems to be such an obstacle to faith for many people, this is a risk worth taking.

My first attempt at writing this chapter reflected our sinful tendency to take responsibility for too much of God's realm above. For some reason, I felt it was necessary to "get God off the hook" by presenting ways in which bad stuff is really part of God's overall good plan for us. It seemed that if I could "take the edge off" bad stuff, then you would exclaim, "Ah! There is no tension in the concept of a good God that allows bad stuff to happen. Therefore, the 'problem' of evil is not really a problem after all!" Well, my line of thinking was garbage, because God does not need me, or anyone else, to get him off the hook. Moreover, trying to explain-away the tension between God who is good and the existence of evil in the world is a pointless task. The tension is there...period.

Why does this tension exist? If God is good, then why are we burdened with sources of pain that strain people with even the strongest faith? Why must we inherit the gigantic national debt and environmental instabilities that loom over our heads? Why do diseases like Cancer, AIDS, and Alzheimer's exist? Why must our lives be subject to skyrocketing random crime and violence? Why must we face tragedies like the Holocaust, untimely deaths of infants and family members, family breakups, and deadly natural disasters? In fact, why doesn't God just completely get rid of all pain, including even death? This "why list" could continue endlessly.

The answer to all of these "why" questions is elusive. The bottom line is that God has not told us why we must live in a tension with bad stuff. We are given some insight into how God is able to use the evil in our world to his glory, but we are not told why God doesn't just take us all to heaven right now, ending pain and suffering for everyone. Does this mean that God is not good? Not at all! It just means that we haven't been able to crawl inside the mind of God and get answers that we don't have. We are tricked into thinking that if we have an explanation for why God allows bad stuff to happen in this world, we have more control. So we engage in various projects, trying to probe into God's realm *above* to find the answers.

God has not revealed the root answers to the "why" questions to us. But even if he did, would that give us any more control? Let's answer this with another question: Do we have any more control over the weather, just because we can predict it (some of the time)? We would like to think we do, but in reality, we don't. We must be wary when people are quick to use hypothetical answers to paint roses on the pain and suffering in our world in the name of God—as if God's existence relies on us having the answers.

So, we don't know why we have bad stuff in our world—just that we have it. Does that mean God's hands are tied? To wrestle with the question "Why does God let bad stuff happen?" let's look briefly at three perspectives, focusing on the third.

First, this question rests on the assumption that pain is evil, and that because God is good and loving, he should ensure a painless life for us. However, this implies that God exists to assist us in our projects supporting pain avoidance. *When we make this assumption, we are projecting our needs onto God, and then we blame God when our projects fail.* Forde speaks directly to this problem:

> A predictable inversion has taken place. We claim freedom in things "above," where we have none, and then blame God for the sorry outcome of things "below," where we have been mandated to take care. We are incensed if anyone asserts that God alone is in charge of things above....We seem quite assured that we have such matters well in hand....Meanwhile, we abdicate from the freedom we have in things below and wonder why God does such a poor job at it.[2]

97

From this we can see that we should not blame God too quickly for all the bad stuff that happens to us.

Second, we must ask, "is it possible that God is actually behind some of the things that we *perceive* to be 'bad'"? Because we will perceive anything that threatens our projects as bad, the answer is "Yes" (but this does not mean God is behind *all* "bad" things). This is often called the *law* or the *wrath of God*, and is something that as sinful creatures, we all need and deserve. To insist on our own projects is to insist on living in the law and having a God of wrath.[3] This is the manner in which God must deal with us when we reject his grace and thus his forgiveness. The good thing, though, is that God will not rest until he has created us anew and we are no longer under his wrath. People no longer under law or wrath are people who have died, been raised, and love and trust God—"when the body and blood are given *to us* and are received in faith."[4] Jesus sacrificed himself for us to restore our relationship with God, ultimately ending God's wrath on us.

It might seem that we're in a dilemma, though, because as fallen creatures in bondage to evil, our perspective is warped. Because we are in bondage, we are likely to confuse God's actions with the devil's. We naturally see anything that threatens our god-projects as evil. Of course, God does intend to threaten our projects! How, then, can we ever keep it all straight? We might think that this spells doom for us.

Without God's action, this certainly does spell doom for us. Fortunately, though, God is a step ahead of us. God's wrath, which we naturally see as evil, actually has a purpose! "So the law was put in charge to lead us to Christ that we might be justified by faith. Now that faith has come, we are no longer under the supervision of the law" (Galatians 3:24-25). God uses his wrath to lead us to Christ. With a little reflection, this makes sense. How could we see a need for God's mercy if we did not have God's wrath? God's wrath serves God's intentions for us. God is at work in some very unexpected places!

The third and most critical understanding of bad stuff is illustrated in the life of a man in the Bible named Joseph. The narrative of Joseph's life is found in Genesis 37-50.

When we meet Joseph, the son of Jacob, he is actually still a boy. Joseph is not on good terms with his older brothers, and the fact that he tattles on them to Jacob does not help. Worsening their relationship is the fact that Jacob seems to favor Joseph and gives him a "richly ornamented robe." Joseph's brothers are understandably jealous. Then, Joseph has a dream. In this dream, his brothers bow down to him. Joseph makes the mistake of telling his brothers about his dream, and of course, they are ticked and hate him even worse. He then has another dream that even the sun, moon, and stars bow down to him. Even his father Jacob rebukes him for this one!

One thing leads to another, and Joseph's brothers devise and execute a plan to get rid of their "dreamer" brother. They throw Joseph into a pit to die and then trick Jacob into believing that Joseph was killed by a wild animal. But seeing a group of slave traders passing by, his brothers change their minds and pull Joseph out of the pit, selling him to the traders. Joseph is eventually purchased by Potiphar—an Egyptian government official. Because the Lord blesses his work, Joseph becomes a respected servant. He is also handsome, which leads Potiphar's wife to "hit" on Joseph. When Joseph refuses her promiscuous advance, she accuses him of attempted rape, and Potiphar has Joseph thrown into the king's prison.

Joseph's good behavior in prison gives him responsibilites over other prisoners, and recognition that eventually allows him to use his God-given ability to accurately interpret a troubling dream of the king's. This leads to Joseph's restoration into service in the kingdom and to great responsibilities. In fact, Joseph becomes the king's "right hand man" and is placed in charge of all of Egypt during a famine. Under Joseph's management, Egypt successfully weathers the famine. In fact, Egypt even has extra grain to sell, which causes Joseph's brothers to travel south to Egypt, and to eventually be reunited with Joseph.

When Joseph reveals himself to his brothers, they are understandably terrified—fearful of revenge. After all, they had sold Joseph into slavery, and here he is now, the most powerful man in the land! But Joseph says to his brothers,

> Do not be distressed and do not be angry with yourselves for selling me here, because it was to save lives that God sent me ahead of you....God sent me ahead of you to preserve a remnant on earth and to save your lives by a great deliverance.
>
> So then, it was not you who sent me here, but God. He made me father to Pharaoh, lord of his entire household and ruler of all Egypt. (Genesis 45:5-8)

Joseph also says to them,

> Don't be afraid. Am I in the place of God? You intended to harm me, but God intended it for good to accomplish what is now being done, the saving of many lives (Genesis 50:19-20).

We can learn a lot about bad stuff from Joseph's journey. First, we can note that he had more than his fair share of hardships! He was thrown into a pit and almost killed by his brothers, but instead they sold him into slavery. After landing in Egypt, he was accused of rape and then imprisoned. He was finally released from prison in order to face a terrible famine. Joseph did not exactly enjoy smooth sailing! The God-given dreams he had shared with has family certainly did not seem to be coming to fruition when he was sold into slavery and imprisoned. Joseph's faith must have been strained during the hard times!

It is in hindsight that Joseph is able to see how God brought good out of his rocky journey—not while he was in the midst of the turmoil! We are never told why Joseph's rise to power took the path it did. Did God plan for Joseph to endure those particular hardships, or was God able to use even people's most evil intentions for good? Or, was it necessary at all for Joseph to endure the hardships that he did? Couldn't God have found a better way? We don't have the final answer to these questions. What we are told is that God fulfilled his promises through Joseph and the events that occurred. At the same time, God reconciled Joseph with his estranged family. Amazing!

God gave Joseph a promise in a dream. Joseph's journey took him through times when that promise must have seemed far-fetched. But as chaotic as the situation may have seemed, God was in control and fulfilled his promise to Joseph. Similarly, God has given you a promise. God has promised you eternal life in his kingdom. This kingdom cannot be shaken. There, God will wipe every tear from your eyes, and there will be no more death or mourning or crying or pain (Revelation 21:4). When we look around at our sometimes hellish surroundings, God's promise may seem far-fetched. We can't help but wonder where God is in the midst of it all. And although we might not see how God is bringing good from our journeys until we are in heaven, God will somehow use the bad stuff in our lives to his glory—guaranteed!

In the meantime, we can continue to drink from the cups of life we have been handed. We can turn toward God—our refuge and our stronghold—trusting that he has our best interest as his goal. If God was inaccessible and hidden, then turning to him would not be much comfort at all. But fortunately for us, in Jesus, God is recklessly and intimately in love with us—so much that it killed him! Jurgen Moltmann observes,

> Christ's sufferings are not exclusive: they are not just his sufferings. They are inclusive—our sufferings too, and the sufferings of the time in which we are living. His cross stands between our crosses...as a sign that God himself participates in our suffering and takes our pains on himself.[5]

Let's now recap what we have found in this chapter. As the popular bumper sticker so boldly proclaims, we all know that "shit happens." Our pain is undeniably real. Yet, we have seen that we might sometimes be too quick to blame God for the bad stuff in our lives. In fact, some bad stuff might only seem bad to us because it threatens our projects. We have also seen that although we are in bondage, God is not. God is not above using whatever material is available, even if this material is a fallen world, to "do himself to us." Joseph's journey in Genesis 37-50 is an excellent example of God's ability to work around evil en-route to reconciliation. As long as we live in an imperfect world, pain will unfortunately be a part of this reconciliation. Often pain seems senseless, sadistic, and purely evil. Even though it often might be, God is God, and he can use even the worst situations toward his good goals.

Yet, God has not revealed to us all the answers. *We cannot pretend to have all the answers about why terrible and painful things happen.* Fortunately for us, Jesus knows about this well! He is our "Wounded Healer."[6] He is present with us in our suffering, experiencing it as we experience it. He bears all our pain—the pain that we would inflict upon ourselves, as well as the pain that we cannot even pretend to explain. God relates with us fully, enabling Jesus to change the seemingly random series of sad incidents and accidents in our lives into a

constant opportunity for faith.[7]   Moltman's insight hits this
home;

> Why God permits all this we do not know. And
> if we did know, it would not help us to live. But if we
> discover where God is, and sense his presence in our
> suffering, then we are at the fountainhead—the source
> out of which life is born anew.[8]

In Jesus, God promises to ultimately take us beyond the bad
stuff in our world. This does not take away our pain, but it does
give us great hope in the midst of it all!

> *God is our refuge and strength, an ever present help in
>   trouble.*
> *Therefore, we will not fear, though the earth give way
>   and the mountains fall into the heart of the sea,*
> *though its waters roar and foam and the mountains
>   quake with their surging.*
>
> *There is a river whose streams make glad the city of
>   God, the holy place where the Most High dwells.*
> *God is within her, she will not fall; God will help her at
>   break of day.*
> *Nations are in uproar, kingdoms fall; he lifts his voice,
>   the earth melts.*
>
> *The Lord Almighty is with us; the God of Jacob is our
>   fortress.*
>
> *Come and see the works of the Lord, the desolations he
>   has brought on the earth.*
> *He makes wars to cease to the ends of the earth; he*

*breaks the bow and shatters the spear, he burns
the shields with fire.*
*Be still and know that I am God; I will be exalted among
the nations, I will be exalted in the earth.*

*The Lord Almighty is with us; The God of Jacob is our
fortress.*

— Psalm 46

Reflections

We all have "bad stuff" in our lives that strains our faith. What is the bad stuff in your life that does this (page 96)?

Do you feel that believing God is good requires us to understand why God allows us to suffer pain (page 96-97)? Why or why not?

Why is it tempting to want an explanation for why God allows us to suffer pain (pages 96-97)?

How is attempting to explain why God allows us to face pain engaging in a project (pages 96-97)?

How is expecting God to keep pain out of our lives pursuing a project (page 97)?

Is everything that seems painful for us really bad? Consider the purpose of God's wrath (pages 98-99).

Are we told why God allowed bad stuff to happen to Joseph (page 101)?

Is there any bad stuff that can possibly thwart the fulfillment of God's promises to you (pages 101-104)?

Chapter Twelve

Intergenerational Rage

It is by offering individuals the opportunity to meld themselves into righteous and hence eternal causes that such political ideologies as Nazism and communism have produced explosions of unparalleled evil in the twentieth century.[1]
— *Ted Peters*

As Joseph's journey was not trouble-free, our journey also has its dark moments. As Generation X, much of the bad stuff in our lives relates to intergenerational tensions in our society. We can rest assured that like Joseph, God will work around these tensions en-route to our reconciliation with each other and with God. In the meantime, we can cling to and find hope in God's promises. Because intergenerational tensions impact us so greatly, it is time that we now peer a little deeper into their implications for GenX.

Why do we have intergenerational tensions? First, let's look at GenX. We feel we are being handed a future over which we are not at the same time handed any control. We are given little elbowroom in which to address our future. We see growing economic and environmental catastrophes looming on the horizon of our maturity. Time is running out. Adding insult to injury is the fact that we are often not given much credibility or respect by our elders. This is largely our plight in a nutshell and as we perceive it, and it causes us anxiety.

Now let's look at our parents' generation—the Boomers. As they are aging, they also worry about their future. However, their worries focus more on having a comfortable retirement including basic social benefits for those who need them. They see that our nation's aging demographics will make it difficult for people of working ages (the post-Boomer generations, including us) to support their retirement. Many are also undoubtedly concerned about the burdens their children will face in the coming years. So, Boomers also have anxiety.

Figure 12-1

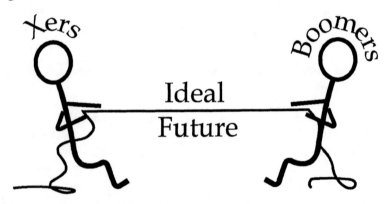

The problem with a troubled future is that it causes anxiety. This anxiety worsens when giving two generations the future for which they dream is not possible because much about their ideal futures conflict. This is our dilemma. We cannot give the large retiring generations the retirement they expect while simultaneously lightening the load on younger generations. The situation feels overwhelming to all generations involved, so we all scramble to gain control over our futures. Their age combined with their size gives Boomers an advantage in this scramble, which heightens intergenerational tensions even more. And while the frenzy continues, we are all anxious. Ironically, when our anxiety increases, our self-concern increases, and the concerns of future generations are again put aside. Both GenX and the Boomers are caught in this cycle.

Although both generations contribute to the tensions, let's now focus more specifically on GenX. The bottom line is that we are anxious about our future and our lack of control over it. Theologian Ted Peters observes, "One sure sign of anxiety over time is the fear of the loss of our future."[2] *Because our identity is so interwoven with our future, we view the death of our future as we would have it as our own death.* In the same way contemplating our physical deaths in this world leads us to engage in death-defying projects, our instinctive move when pondering the death of our future is also toward projects. What is our project of choice? Springing from the thought of Becker, Peters says that when responding to our consciousness of death, we often create the illusion that we can attain immortality.

> If we find cannot accept our own death with grace, we may embark on a path of self-delusion, painting a picture of ourselves as immortal. In this delusionary state, beset by rising frustration and rage, we may seek to create our own immortality by stealing life from others.[3]

As our rage over intergenerational tensions rises, we might think we can increase our own power by stealing it from our favorite scapegoat—the Boomers. We might harbor resentments, voice negative or slanderous comments, and maybe even participate in outright rebellion. Such actions are similar to an insecure child on a playground trying to find power in life by bad-mouthing other children or by bullying them for their lunch money. While "killing" others seems to relieve our own fear of being killed, it is only an illusion. "The key link in the logic of this cultural illusion is the mistaken belief that we can transfer life from one being to another." [4]

This is the flag of caution I must raise to our generation. I grant that as a generation we feel raped as the inheritors of a problematic future. And I hope that we will dive-in and do what we can to salvage our future. But we must take note that "anxiety makes loving difficult, sometimes impossible."[5] We must beware that "the threat of death and the need for survival put our nervous fingers on the trigger of the weapon of sin."[6] We must realize how, "in our attempts to gain victory over evil, we can so easily increase evil."[7] Regardless of their attitude toward us, we must seek to work with other generations—not against them.

It might help us to remember that Jesus did not live and die only for Generation X. Through Jesus, God came to reconcile the whole world to himself because he loves the world (see John 3:16-17). The word "world" in our English Bible translations is translated from the Greek word "cosmos." In Colossians 1:20, Paul reiterates that through Jesus, God is pleased to reconcile "all things" to himself. If God loves the cosmos, then God loves Boomers too.

We can say, then, that God is omnigenerational. We sometimes use other "omni" words to describe God such as "omniscient" (all-knowing) and "omnipotent" (all-powerful). Omnigenerational, then, means all-generational. All generations together, including Xers and Boomers, make-up the body of Christ. In 1 Corinthians 12, Paul reminds us of our diversity (see also Romans 12:4-5):

> The body is a unit, though it is made up of many parts; and though all its parts are many, they form one

110

body. So it is with Christ....God has arranged the parts in the body, every one of them, just as he wanted them to be. If they were all one part, where would the body be? As it is, there are many parts, but one body.

In the same way that each person brings different gifts to the body of Christ, so does each generation. With this in mind, we are wise to work together, finding strength in our diversity rather than weakness. Surely this won't be easy, but who said it would be? Such intergenerational cooperation will require huge measures of grace, forgiveness, self-sacrifice, and hard work. James Gambone, a facilitator of intergenerational dialogue, offers the following:

> The idea of promoting intergenerational respect, caring and cooperation offers a real alternative to the current secular self-interest, "we-they" attitudes. Wouldn't our national dialogue on race, welfare reform and morality be significantly different if we first agreed to have the interests of all generations laid out clearly on the table? Wouldn't the quality of our religious dialogues improve significantly if all generations agreed to be respectful, caring and cooperative? And wouldn't the depth of the issues we all face as a society increase in significance if someone represented the interests of those who cannot speak for themselves and those yet unborn?[8]

There is no quick, easy way out of our dilemma. But we can rest assured that like Joseph, God will work in and around our intergenerational tensions and our tenuous future en-route to our reconciliation with each other. As God works to close the chasms dividing us, let's begin looking for Christ in each other. And although we don't know exactly when full intergenerational reconciliation will happen, let's pray that it happens today. In the meantime, we can cling to and find hope in God's promises.

Reflections

Why do both Xers and Boomers have anxiety about their futures (pages 107-108)?

What is our temptation as we face our anxiety about our future? In other words, what might this anxiety cause us to do (pages 109-110)?

How might we try to steal life from Boomers (pages 109-110)?

What positives might we find in our generational differences from others (pages 110-111)?

Why is good intergenerational dialogue vital to our future (page 111)?

Chapter Thirteen

Life with God

> Grace is rather the power of God revealed in Christ which destroys the *un*natural, destroys man's refusal to be natural. Grace thus makes nature what it was intended to be. In that sense grace perfects nature—not because it adds what was lacking, but precisely because it makes nature to be nature once again. The grace of God is a power strong enough to make and keep us human.[1]
>
> *— Gerhard Forde*

This quotation from Forde says a lot! Through Christ's identification with us, his death, and his resurrection, we are now free to be creatures in God's *good* creation. Only when we receive creation back as a gift can we rejoice in it.[2] In Romans 6:4-5, Paul says:

> We were therefore buried with him through baptism into death in order that, just as Christ was raised from the dead through the glory of the Father, we too might live a new life.

We have been buried with him in baptism and are reborn as the creatures he created us to be. God is no longer our project. Instead, we are God's. Even better, we have become God's children. We are finally satisfied to be in God's image, tending the garden he has given us to care for, as God also cares for us.

This is wonderful, freeing news. Yet, we would be naive to think that Christian life is pure bliss. Even as a new creation, we still live in tension (often it's more like a battle) with our old selves that want to remain in the driver's seat. In Forde's words, "The old Adam has been drowned in the waters of baptism, but he is a good swimmer!"[3] The old Adam clings to our nature all the way to our earthly grave[4]—but that is where he is finally defeated. As the old Adam continues to cling to us, we must cling to the promise of our death and resurrection in Christ. Jesus reminds us that being his disciple means following him through crucifixion (see Luke 14:27). Doing this one time and then leaving it in the past is not enough—it must be a daily event.

From this, we can discern three things about our new life with God. *First*, as we have noted, it's not sheer bliss. Too often, people are misled into believing that the Christian life is easy—that all that we need to do to have our problems disappear is to "become a Christian," or something like that. This is when our "crap detectors" should let out piercing warnings. To fall into this trap is to believe that the kingdom of heaven in all its fullness has already arrived. If we open our eyes to the world around us, though, we might venture to say that it looks more like hell than like heaven!

Kierkegaard illustrates that life with God cannot be easy by having us imagine that we lived in Jesus' time.[5] So, let's try it. Imagine yourself living near Jesus two thousand years ago. Now, meet Jesus. He's a man who prefers the company of sinners, lepers (also considered to be sinners) lunatics, the poor, and the miserable. Because of his associations and some of his words and actions, he was scorned as a deceiver and blasphemer. Word is spreading through the grapevine that he is to be tried and killed as a criminal.

Not exactly the kind of company most parents would want their children to keep! Worse, he wants your company! He specifically seeks you out to be his companion, and sends you a gift. As the FedEx driver arrives (they had FedEx back then, didn't they?) and hands you your gift, your neighbor arrives home. Your neighbor, by the way, is the county judge. He is curious and wanders over to look at your package, which, to your dismay, has "From Jesus" scrawled across it in big letters. Bummer! He realizes that your unsolicited gift came from Jesus and immediately judges you to be guilty by association. Your future suddenly looks grim. Kierkegaard observes that truly being a Christian is in human eyes to mean suffering every possible evil, every mockery and insult, and finally to be punished as a criminal.[6] Such persecution is a natural, defensive reaction of project-pursuers who, in the face of a free gift, fear the realization of the insignificance and ultimate futility of their own projects. As people who have had projects, we should know!

So, your neighbor has seen your gift. At this point, many people depart on long emotional tangents about what you might do—whether you will admit to your association with Jesus or not. As important as we might think giving the right answer is, the truth of the matter is that it does not affect Jesus' decision for you. Sure, it would be nice if you would claim him as your friend, but when it gets right down to it, we will likely do exactly what Jesus' disciples did—run like the wind! While Jesus hung dying on a cross, they were hiding in a locked room. But Jesus returned, found them in their locked room, and said "Peace be with you" (Luke 24:36).

The Church is a place for sinners—a community of the faithful for whom the natural instinct is to flee from God. Jesus recognizes our dilemma. That is, after all, why he bothered to sacrifice himself for us. Although people in the Church are no longer fully in bondage, we are still caught in the middle of a powerful battle. Yet, we live in the shadow of the cross—we are under God's grace. Fallout from this still-raging battle may more often than not cause the Church to look hypocritical to the rest of the world. This is largely due to the misunderstanding (often perpetuated by well meaning but misdirected Christians) that Christians should represent some certain level of perfection. However, the reality is that all Christians sin! Christians are rightly perceived as hypocritical when we claim to be sinless. But when we admit to our sin before others and before God, this hypocrisy disappears. Living in this tension of God's freeing grace vs. our sinful inclinations is only possible because God is merciful. Fortunately, the grace of God is where those who labor and are burdened find rest. And though the battle may rage for a little longer, the war has already been won.

The *second* important thing that we can discern about our new life with God is that when we bask in our faithful relationship with God, it is our privilege and joy to respond to God's grace in our lives. This response is similar to the response of two people who have fallen in love. Their love for each other will fuel spontaneous acts of kindness for each other that would have never happened had the love not existed. These acts do not stop with gifts of nice words and nice things to each other. The two people in love have a sacrificial relationship. They walk together so closely that to serve the other is no different than to serve themselves. Sharing the unpleasant aspects of life together, being willing to help the other remove a wart that they can't reach, risking illness to care for the other when they're ill, and even being willing to sacrifice your life to save the other, are all responses found in couples in love.

All we need to do is look at Christ's sacrifice on the cross to say, without hesitation, that God is in love with us. As with any relationship, before this love is mutual we will likely feel smothered by the love of the other. Probably we will try to ignore or flee the situation. But when the love becomes mutual, the spontaneous acts of kindness and service are endless. We can't help but respond to the love. As children of God, our love relationship has huge implications. Jesus says,

> Then the righteous will answer him, "Lord, when did we see you hungry and feed you, or thirsty and give you something to drink? When did we see you a stranger and invite you in, or needing clothes and clothe you? When did we see you sick or in prison and visit you?
> The King will reply, "I tell you the truth, whatever you did for one of the least of these brothers of mine, you did for me." (Matthew 25:37-40)

In our new relationship with Christ, our response will be to praise God, our lover, for who he is. We will also serve God. Because a love relationship causes spontaneous acts of kindness and service, responding to our relationship with God also entails responding with kindness and service to the needs of others. As Christ has come to us, we will go into the garden God has given us and "be Christ" to our brothers and sisters. We will share God's words of love and hope, feed the poor, care for the elderly, help the sick, visit the imprisoned, and care for the environment. We will hurdle intergenerational tensions and divisions. Labels like "Generation X" and "Baby Boomers" will disappear in favor of one label for all--"Children of God." Generations yet unborn will have a voice in our present actions and strategic planning.

All these things and more will not occur out of obligation, but out of love and in the name of Christ. They are not accomplished as our own god-projects, but as a result of being God's project. God has taken us through death, resurrected us into new life, and thrust us back into the garden to care for it. We have been reborn into this world as God's children. With death conquered and the fear of death gone, our fear of life disappears too![7] We no longer feel paralyzed by our future. Instead, we are filled with hope for our world! The Christian community is one of "support, celebration, and affirmation in which we can engage the world and lift up what has already begun in us."[8] As part of this community, GenX is poised to dampen the reactionary pendulum swinging between generations and to restore a balance built on God's love. We are God's agents of change in the garden. Yet, as we move forward in our Christian lives, we must remember that because we continue to live in a world of tension, we will remain far short of finding ourselves in a perfect world—but it will certainly be "the end of the world as we know it!"

The *third* and most important thing we can discern about our new life with God is indeed the fact that we have hope in God's final victory over death and the devil. In this final time, God *will* take us beyond our world of tension, imperfection, and pain. This hope is not rooted in ourselves or in our god-projects of life. Likewise, we have no hope in our apathy, in our efforts to not have projects, or in efforts to transcend our uncomfortable realities. The bottom line is that these and all efforts are really nothing but futile projects. Rather, *our hope lies in Jesus' complete identification with us, his sacrifice for us, and his promise that we will follow him into an eternity with our loving creator.* Without God's amazing promise to us, how are we to meet life's inevitable challenges, pain, and tragedies head-on?

We Xers have not been placed on an easy path to trod. We possibly will never enjoy a standard of living comparable to our parents'. Our future undoubtedly holds dark moments. But in the light Jesus, we have a quality of life that is unparalleled. Society's measurements of living standards and success in this life are irrelevant in the face of God's gift of eternal life. The one true source of life has given life back to us. So we trust in God, knowing that God is waiting for us, that God is hoping for us, and that we are invited to God's future. Trusting our future to God is the essence of faithful living. This faith will carry us through our future in this world, through our physical death and resurrection, and into the glorious presence of our creator. We are holding in our hands the most marvelous invitation we have ever had.[9] This, more than anything, gives us incredible hope!

Reflections

What is the significance of our baptism in our life with God (pages 115-116)?

What is our "old Adam" and how does he/she cause tension in our lives (pages 63,116)?

Why is it that, as Christians, we can expect to be persecuted in various ways (page 117)?

What causes Christians to be or appear hypocritical (page 118)?

Consider some ways you think the Church and its members might fall into hypocrisy today?

How does Christ's sacrificial death demonstrate God's love for us (pages 118-119)?

Have you ever felt smothered by God's love (pages 118-119)? When?

What are ways that the Church and its members respond to God's grace (page 119-120)?

How might you be able to respond to God's grace in your life?

What does it mean to "be Christ" to our neighbors (page 119)?

As you continue to live your life in tension in this imperfect world, where is your hope?

Appendix

Resources...

For information on intergenerational dialog, see Dr. James Gambone, *Together for Tomorrow: Building Community Through Intergenerational Dialogue*, Available through Elder Eye Press, 800-586-9054.

For information on the Intentional Intergenerational Ministry (IIM) Movement, visit the IIM website at *www.intgenmin.com* or see Dr. James Gambone, *All Are Welcome: A Primer for Intentional Intergenerational Ministry and Dialogue,* Available in the IIM Starter Kit from Lutheran Brotherhood, 800-688-6067 and from Elder Eye Press, 800-586-9054.

For a straightforward and digestible introduction to reading the Bible, see: Craig R. Koester, *A Beginner's Guide to Reading the Bible* (Minneapolis: Augsburg Fortress, 1991).

For an overview of different world views influencing our world, see: James W. Sire, *The Universe Next Door* (Downer's Grove: InterVarsity Press, 1988).

For an overview of different denominations and religious groups found within the United States, see the most current edition of: Frank S. Mead, *Handbook of Denominations in the United States*, Abingdon Press.

Following is a suggested reading list for those interested in examining arguments supporting the reasonableness of Christianity:

Winfried Corduan, *Reasonable Faith: Basic Christian Apologetics* (Nashville: Broadman & Holman Publishers, 1993).

J. P. Moreland, *Scaling the Secular City: A Defense of Christianitiy* (Grand Rapids: Baker Book House, 1987).

Timothy R. Phillips and Dennis L. Okholm, eds., *Christian Apologetics in the Postmodern World* (Downers Grove: InterVarsity Press, 1995).

For an especially interesting and unique argument on behalf of Christianity (commonly known as *Pascal's Wager*), see: Blaise Pascal, *Pensées*, translation and introduction by A.J. Krailsheimer (New York: Penguin Books USA, Inc., 1995) 418/233, P. 121-125. You can also easily find this argument quoted on the World Wide Web.

Notes

Introduction:

[1] Tim Celek, Dieter Zander, and Patrick Kampert, *Inside the Soul of a New Generation:Insights and Strategies for Reaching Busters* (Grand Rapids: Zondervan, 1996), 20.

Chapter 1: "What's the Point?"

[1] Henri J. M. Nouwen, *The Wounded Healer* (New York: Doubleday, 1972), 6-7.
[2] Deiter Zander, "The Gospel for Generation X," *Leadership* 16 (Spring 1995): 38.
[3] Susan A. MacManus, *Young v. Old: Generational Combat in the 21st Century*, (Westview Press, 1996), 3-25, quoted in Richard D. Thau and Jay S. Heflin, eds., *Generations Apart: Xers vs. Boomers vs. the Elderly* (Amherst, New York: Prometheus Books, 1997), 32.
[4] See Robert A. George "Stuck in the Shadows with You: Observations on Post-Boomer Culture," quoted in Richard D. Thau and Jay S. Heflin, eds., *Generations Apart*, 24-30.
[5] Lester C. Thurow, "The Birth of a Revolutionary Class," *New York Times Magazine* (May 19, 1996): 46-47, quoted in Richard D. Thau and Jay S. Heflin, eds., *Generations Apart*, 34-35.
[6] Jurgen Moltmann, *Jesus Christ for Today's World*, trans. Margaret Kohl (Minneapolis: Fortress Press, 1994), 26-27.
[7] Deiter Zander, "The Gospel for Generation X," 37.
[8] Ibid.
[9] See Robert A. George "Stuck in the Shadows with You: Observations on Post-Boomer Culture," 28.
[10] Andres Tapia, "Reaching the First Post-Christian Generation: Raised in a world of MTV, AIDS, and a trillion dollar debt, Generation X is

making new demands on the church," *Christianity Today* 38 (12 September 1994): 19.

[11] See Robert A. George "Stuck in the Shadows with You: Observations on Post-Boomer Culture," 25.

[12] Ibid., 30.

[13] Lester C. Thurow, "The Birth of a Revolutionary Class," 35.

[14] Andres Tapia, "Reaching the First Post-Christian Generation," 19.

[15] Tim Celek, Dieter Zander, and Patrick Kampert, *Inside the Soul of a New Generation*, 71.

Chapter 2: "Projects"

[1] Friedrich Schleiermacher, *On Religion: Speeches to Its Cultured Despisers*, trans. John Oman, with a foreword by Jack Forstman (Louisville: Westminster/John Knox Press, 1994), 2.

[2] Blaise Pascal, *Pensées*, translation and introduction by A.J. Krailsheimer (New York: Penguin Books USA, Inc., 1995) 70/165b, p. 19.

[3] Ernest Becker, *The Denial of Death* (New York: The Free Press, 1973), 16.

[4] Ibid., 58.

[5] Ibid., 26.

[6] Ibid., 87.

[7] This comparison was given to me by two of my friends and sounding boards for this book, Tony and Lisa Kim.

Chapter 3: "Transcendence"

[1] Includes excerpts from Blaise Pascal, *Pensées*, 136/139, pp. 37-39.

[2] This analogy was given to me by my colleague, Brian Mundt.

[3] John Dominic Crossan, *The Dark Interval: Towards a Theology of Story*, 1st ed. (Niles, IL:Argus Communications, 1975), 45-46.

[4] Blaise Pascal, *Pensées*, 136/139, P. 41.

[5] Douglas Groothuis, *The Soul in Cyberspace* (Grand Rapids: Baker Books, 1997), 28.

[6] Ernest Becker, *The Denial of Death*, 178.

[7] Ibid., 193.

Chapter 4: "Falling Upward"

[1] Martin Luther, *The Bondage of the Will* in *Luther's Works*, vol. 33, *Career of the Reformer III*, ed. and trans. Philip S. Watson (Philadelphia: Fortress Press, 1972), P 175-176.
[2] Gerhard Forde, *Theology is for Proclamation* (Minneapolis: Augsburg Fortress, 1990), 48–49.
[3] Martin Luther, *The Bondage of the Will*, 65.
[4] Ibid., 272.

Chapter 5: "Is God Relevant?"

[1] Tony Campolo, *The Kingdom of God is a Party* (Dallas: Word Publishing, 1990), 46-47.

Chapter 6: "The Accident"

[1] Gerhard Forde, *The Work of Christ*, from *Christian Dogmatics*, ed. Carl E. Braaten and Robert W. Jenson (Philadelphia: Fortress Press, 1984), 88.
[2] Ibid., 89.
[3] Ibid., 91-92.
[4] Gerhard Forde, *Where God Meets Man: Luther's Down-to-Earth Approach to the Gospel* (Minneapolis: Augsburg Publishing House, 1972), 37.
[5] Ibid., 39.
[6] Ibid., 43.
[7] Ibid., 39.
[8] Ibid., 40.
[9] Martin Luther, *The Small Catechism* (Minneapolis: Augsburg Publishing House, 1979), 25.

Chapter 7: "The Offense"

[1] Soren Kierkegaard, *Practice in Christianity*, ed. Howard V. Hong and Edna H. Hong (Princeton, N.J.: Princeton University Press, 1991), 78.

[2] Ibid., 86.

[3] Some attributes listed are from: Andres Tapia, "Reaching the First Post-Christian Generation...", 23.

[4] *Book of Concord: The Confessions of the Evangelical Lutheran Church*, ed. and trans. Theodore G. Tappert (Philadelphia: Fortress Press, 1959), 365.

[5] Soren Kierkegaard, *Practice in Christianity*, 91.

[6] Henri J. M. Nouwen, *The Path of Power* (New York: Crossroad Publishing Company, 1995), 20.

[7] Ibid., 18.

[8] Henri J. M. Nouwen, *The Path of Waiting* (New York: Crossroad Publishing Company, 1995), 44.

[9] Gerhard Forde, Systematic Theology Course Lecture at Luther Seminary, St. Paul, Minnesota, 7 May 1997.

Chapter 8: "Faith and Grace"

[1] C. S. Lewis, *Mere Christianity* (New York: Macmillan Publishing Company, 1952), 110.

[2] *Book of Concord*, 30.

[3] Leif Grane, *The Augsburg Confession: A Commentary*, trans. John H. Rasmussen (Minneapolis: Augsburg Publishing House, 1987), 60-61.

[4] Gerhard Forde, *Theology is for Proclamation*, 141.

[5] This marriage analogy was suggested by my colleague, Roy Noel.

[6] *Luther's Works*, vol. 54, *Table Talk*, ed. and trans. Theodore G. Tappert (Philadelphia: Fortress Press, 1967), No. 138, P. 20.

Chapter 9: "Three Parables"

[1] Partially paraphrased from *Table Talk*, No. 5580a, P. 456.

[2] These parables are also treated together in Jurgen Moltmann, *Jesus Christ for Today's World*, 11-12.

Chapter 10: "Naaman"

[1] *Calvin's Institutes: A New Compend*, ed. Hugh T. Kerr (Louisville: Westminster/John Knox Press, 1989), III.xi.18, P. 102.

Chapter 11: "Bad Stuff"

[1] Wayne E. Oates, *Grief, Transition, and Loss: A Pastor's Practical Guide* (Minneapolis: Fortress Press, 1997), 83.

[2] Gerhard Forde, *Theology is for Proclamation*, 118.

[3] Gerhard Forde, *The Work of Christ*, 58.

[4] Ibid., 51.

[5] Jurgen Moltmann, *Jesus Christ for Today's World*, 39.

[6] The title of an excellent work by Henri J. M. Nouwen, *The Wounded Healer* (New York: Doubleday, 1972).

[7] Henri J. M. Nouwen, *Out of Solitude* (Notre Dame, Indiana: Ave Maria Press, 1974), 55.

[8] Jurgen Moltmann, *Jesus Christ for Today's World*, 46.

Chapter 12: "Intergenerational Rage"

[1] Ted Peters, *Sin: Radical Evil in Soul and Society* (Grand Rapids: Eerdmans, 1994), 54.

[2] Ibid., 37.

[3] Ted Peters, *Sin*, 35.

[4] Ernest Becker paraphrased in Ted Peters, *Sin*, 52.

[5] Ted Peters, *Sin*, 20.

[6] Ibid.

[7] Ernest Becker paraphrased in Ted Peters, *Sin*, 53.

[8] James V. Gambone, *A Primer for Intentional Intergenerational Ministry and Dialogue* (Crystal Bay, MN: Elder Eye Press, 1998), vii.

Chapter 13: "Life with God"

[1] Gerhard Forde, *Where God Meets Man*, 56-57.

[2] Ibid., 58.

[3] Gerhard Forde, Systematic Theology Course Lecture at Luther Seminary, St. Paul, Minnesota, 12 May 1997.

[4] *Book of Concord*, 565, 567.

[5] Soren Kierkegaard, *Practice in Christianity*, 52.

[6] Ibid., 106.

[7] Jurgen Moltmann, *Jesus Christ for Today's World*, 87.
[8] Henri J. M. Nouwen, *The Path of Waiting*, 24.
[9] Jurgen Moltmann, *Jesus Christ for Today's World*, 132.

Index

HOW TO ORDER

For you convenience, you may order this book directly from the publisher. Please visit the Tekna Books web site for current pricing and ordering instructions.

www.teknabooks.com

TEKNA BOOKS

HOW TO ORDER

For you convenience, you may order this book directly from the publisher. Please visit the Tekna Books web site for current pricing and ordering instructions.

www.teknabooks.com

TEKNA BOOKS